WHITE
EMPRESSES

AND OTHER CANADIAN PACIFIC LINERS
OF THE 1920s & 30s

WHITE EMPRESSES

AND OTHER CANADIAN PACIFIC LINERS OF THE 1920s & 30s

WILLIAM H. MILLER

FONTHILL

Once again, to my dear friend Tony La Forgia,
who has continuously helped me in so many ways

Front cover: Painting of the *Duchess of York* departing from Bermuda. (*Stephen Card*)

Fonthill Media Language Policy

Fonthill Media publishes in the international English language market. One language edition is published worldwide. As there are minor differences in spelling and presentation, especially with regard to American English and British English, a policy is necessary to define which form of English to use. The Fonthill Policy is to use the form of English native to the author. William H. Miller was born and educated in the United States; therefore American English has been adopted in this publication.

Fonthill Media Limited
Fonthill Media LLC
www.fonthillmedia.com
office@fonthillmedia.com

First published in the United Kingdom and the United States of America 2018

British Library Cataloguing in Publication Data:
A catalogue record for this book is available from the British Library

Copyright © William H. Miller 2018

ISBN 978-1-78155-672-6

Typeset in 11pt on 13pt Minion Pro
Printed and bound in England

CONTENTS

Acknowledgments   6

Introduction   7

  1   Pacific Empresses   9

  2   Ships on the Atlantic   28

  3   Sturdy Ships: Four Duchesses   50

  4   Speed Queen of the Pacific   65

  5   The Greatest & Grandest Empress   83

Bibliography   112

ACKNOWLEDGMENTS

Like building and then manning one of these Canadian Pacific passenger liners, many hands were involved in the production of this book. I am more of the coordinator from a sort of literary wheelhouse. First of all, my thanks to Alan Sutton and Jay Slater of Fonthill Media, and to their fine team, for taking on this project and seeing it through completion.

Other first-class hands that have assisted include Richard Faber, Michael Hadgis, Norman Knebel, Anthony La Forgia, and Stephen Card. Special thanks to fellow author Les Streater for his assistance with rare, but many very useful photos. Further, but important assistance—long-serving crew members—came from Ernest Arroyo, Alf Batchelder, Michael Cassar, the late Frank Cronican, Richard de Kerbrech, the late Alex Duncan, the late John Gillespie, David Hutchings, the late Alice Keppel-Thomas, Tim Noble, the late C. M. Squarey, the late Everett Viez, Albert Wilhelmi, and David Williams. Organizations that have assisted include Canadian Pacific Steamships, Cunard Line, Port Authority of New York & New Jersey, Steamship Historical Society of America, World Ocean & Cruise Liner Society, and World Ship Society. Any omissions are sincerely regretted.

INTRODUCTION

Indeed, an interesting collection of ships, but unfortunately I missed all of them. They were before my time—except indirectly for the *Empress of Japan*. Through my grandmother's kindness and generosity, I had my very first cruise on the *Hanseatic* in November 1961. The *Hanseatic* had been the *Empress of Japan* and later the *Empress of Scotland*. As I recall from that long-ago voyage, the ship still retained some of her earlier Canadian Pacific décor: the department store-like revolving doors onto the Promenade Deck stand out in memory, as does the orchestra gallery above the main dining room.

Canadian Pacific had a great fleet of liners. Of course, I well remember the post-war liners, the last three—the *Empress of Britain*, *Empress of England*, and *Empress of Canada*. Yet the company's pre-war passenger ships were more diverse—big liners as well as smaller ones.

That pre-war fleet, in my opinion, was dominated by the four *Empress* liners on the Pacific, the quartet of Duchess ships, the *Empress of Japan* and, the "super star" of the fleet, the exceptional *Empress of Britain*. She was pure 1930s dreamboat. The exterior of the *Empress of Britain*—capped by her three, oversized buff funnels and having a white hull—was pure ocean liner perfection. She ranked, again in my opinion, as one of the best-looking liners of the '30s, joining the likes of the *Conte di Savoia*, the *Nieuw Amsterdam*, the second *Mauretania*, the *Andes*, and, although due in 1940, the *Queen Elizabeth*. Each seemed to have just the right balance, just the right touches. Inside, the *Empress of Britain* was pure luxury, mostly Deco luxury: her Cathay Lounge was exceptional and was classed by some as being Chinese or Asian Deco. Other public rooms and her suites were nothing short of being superb.

Canadian Pacific also created some of the finest, most evocative posters of '20s and '30s travel. The images stir the desire to travel, to go to sea, to enjoy an Atlantic crossing, see exotic, faraway places, or escape to sun-drenched, warm weather. The company also produced some of the most extravagant, well-illustrated booklets and brochures for its liner services. I myself am delighted to own an original poster from the '30s, colorfully depicting the *Empress of Japan* inbound with a Chinese oarsman and his junk (Chinese sailing craft) in the foreground. I sometimes sit and stare—and then dream of sailing off to Hong Kong or Shanghai.

Of course, the less-remembered Canadian Pacific ships—like the *Alsatian* and the "M" class—are interesting. Again, in this book, they too see the light of day.

At times when writing this book, I could almost see the *Empress of Japan* speeding across the Pacific, the *Empress of Russia* berthed at Yokohama, and, better still, the *Empress of Britain* arriving in Bombay during one of her world cruises. Yes, Canadian Pacific in the '20s and '30s spanned the world. In this book, they are to reappear in a grand review. The passengers are aboard, tugs prepare for a sailing, and those mighty whistles are sounding.

Bill Miller
Secaucus, New Jersey
Summer 2017

1

PACIFIC EMPRESSES

Style and grace: The handsome *Empress of Russia* arriving at Vancouver. (*Alex Duncan*)

The *Empress of Russia* loading at Vancouver. (*ALF collection*)

Bon voyage: Outbound at Vancouver in 1938. (*Alex Duncan*)

Above left: Speed was very important—Canadian Pacific was fastest to the distant Orient. (*Les Streater collection*)

Above right: Off to ports such as Yokohama, Kobe, and Shanghai. (*Les Streater collection*)

The *Empress of Russia*

Some travel pundits said that the very finest liner service on the Pacific was maintained by Canadian Pacific, the passenger ship arm of that great Anglo-Canadian travel empire (the company also had trains, hotels, small steamers and freighters, and a separate Atlantic liner fleet). Instead of the Suez Canal, Canadian Pacific offered an alternate route to the Orient: crossing the Atlantic from Britain by liner, then across Canada by rail, and finally across the Pacific by other company passenger liners. From Vancouver and nearby Victoria, it was five days to Honolulu, nine days to Yokohama, ten to Kobe, twelve to Shanghai, fifteen days to Hong Kong, and seventeen days to Manila. First-class fares in 1929 were posted as $120 to Honolulu, $310 to Japan, and $350 to China. European servants could accompany passengers for an entire one-way voyage for $110; Asian servants were charged $50. On the lower decks, there were dormitory quarters in third class, with fares, say, from Shanghai to Vancouver of $115 with European food and $85 with Oriental food.

On July 20, 1911, the *Empress of China* was wrecked near Yokohama. This was a blow to Canadian Pacific's trans-Pacific operations. Then there was an added blow: it was the same year that Japan's Toyo Yusen introduced a trio of brand-new express liners on their run to California. To counteract, Canadian Pacific ordered two new liners for its Pacific service out of Vancouver and Victoria. Introduced in 1913, the two new liners, the *Empress of Russia* and the *Empress of Asia*, were quickly acclaimed as the finest liners on the Pacific. Indeed, Canadian Pacific had made the right decision.

After World War I, in 1921, a third ship, the former German *Empress of Australia*, was added and then, a year later, the *Empress of Canada* was built and so completed the Pacific quartet.

Consequently, the four noted Canadian Pacific liners of the '20s were all three-stackers: the superb collection of the *Empress of Russia*, the *Empress of Asia*, the *Empress of Australia*, and the *Empress of Canada*. This ship and her twin sister, the *Empress of Asia*, were the largest, fastest and most luxurious to date for trans-Pacific service. Built by Fairfields of Glasgow, the 16,810-ton *Empress of Russia* was launched on August 28, 1912. She had steam turbine drive, sixty-four furnaces, could make 19 knots, and her bunkers could hold over 4,600 tons of coal. The maximum passenger capacity was 1,192, divided between 284 first class, 100 second, and 808 in so-called Asiatic steerage.

Delivered in April 1913, she then set off on a long delivery voyage from Liverpool to Hong Kong via Suez. On her very first Pacific voyage, beginning on May 21, she immediately established a speed record, one that stood for nine years. She made Hong Kong to Vancouver via Nagasaki in eight days and eighteen hours. Instantly, she was a successful and soon very popular ship.

In the summer of 1914, the onset of World War I in Europe changed everything. Requisitioned by the Admiralty at Vancouver, she was ordered to Hong Kong, outfitted with guns, and then sent off for Indian Ocean armed merchant cruiser duties. Later, in 1915 and based at Aden, she served as a guard ship at the Red Sea. Ironically, her companion guard ship was her sister, the *Empress of Asia*. She left the high heat of the Red Sea in 1918, however, for trooping duties on the North Atlantic, including voyages from New York. Two months after the war ended, in January 1919, the *Empress of Russia* was released and left on a long voyage to Hong Kong, where she was refitted for further commercial service. On March 8, she was officially handed back to Canadian Pacific and resumed trans-ocean voyages. In all, from 1913 until 1940, she would make 310 Pacific voyages. Painted with a traditional black hull, she and her fleet mates were repainted with a white hull and a yellow band in 1927.

Increasingly, in the 1930s, however, Canadian Pacific faced greater competition on the trans-Pacific run from the likes of America's Dollar Line and Japan's NYK Line. The company was prompted, of course, to strengthen their own operation with the 26,000-grt *Empress of Japan* (qv) (listed in Chapter 4), added in 1930 and soon established as the fastest liner on the Pacific.

Just as with World War I, World War II changed everything. Although she continued for a year after Britain entered the hostilities (on September 3, 1939), the *Empress of Russia* was requisitioned— for a second time—and stripped of her peacetime fittings and then outfitted at Vancouver. In February, she was off on a long voyage to Glasgow for further use as a troopship. A notation came in October 1943 when she repatriated British prisoners of war from Stockholm.

Worn and tired at war's end, she was in desperate need of a refit, but while at the Vickers' yard at Barrow, on September 8, 1945, she was destroyed in a flash fire. At thirty-two years of age, she was beyond economic repair. Her fire-gutted remains were cut-up locally at Barrow.

The *Empress of Asia*

Launched on November 23, 1912, at Glasgow, the 16,909-ton *Empress of Asia* was delivered in May 1913 and set off a month later from Liverpool to Hong Kong via the South African Cape. She too was a quick success on the Pacific, but then was called to war duties in August 1914. Outfitted as an armed merchant cruiser, she later joined her sister out in the Red Sea, but for a short time. In 1916, she returned to Canadian Pacific service from Vancouver, but under wartime standards for a British-flag ship. In May 1918, she was given different orders: she was sent from Vancouver to New York via Panama for trans-Atlantic trooping services. In all, she made six voyages between New York and Europe.

In 1919, it was time to return to the Pacific, and on January 2, she departed Liverpool for the long voyage to Hong Kong. Later refitted to her luxurious self, she had a long, dependable life with little notation. On January 11, 1926, she rammed and sank the Indo-China Steam Navigation Company's steamer *Tung Shing* and then she too was repainted in all-white in 1927.

On January 1, 1941, at the completion of her 307th voyage, she was requisitioned for war duties at Vancouver, but a year later, there was tragedy. On February 5, 1942, the *Empress of Asia* was attacked and sunk in Pacific waters off Singapore by no less than twenty-seven Japanese bombers. With 2,651 onboard, it was miraculous that all but nineteen survived. A number of survivors in lifeboats made their way to Java, but most of them were later captured by the Japanese and imprisoned.

The *Empress of Asia* departing for the Orient. (*ALF collection*)

The *Empress of Australia*

The *Empress of Australia*, a 21,860-tonner, was perhaps the most noted and famous of this quartet of Pacific Empress liners of the '20s. She had been a ship of reparations, coming to the company after World War I. She was partially built as the *Tirpitz* for Hamburg-America Line in 1913–14, but never completed owing to the outbreak of war. It was said she would be the review ship when the Kaiser accepted the defeated British naval fleet. She sat incomplete throughout the hostilities; in 1919, she was ceded to Britain as reparations and then to Canadian Pacific. She became the *Empress of Australia* a year later, with finished accommodations for 1,513 passengers—404 in first class, 165 second class, 270 third class, and 674 steerage. Generally known as the flagship of the "Pacific Empresses," the *Empress of Australia* was also a heroic ship. She rescued over 2,000 people from the Great Kantō earthquake, which occurred on September 1, 1923.

In 1930, following the arrival of the bigger, faster, and more luxurious *Empress of Japan*, the *Empress of Australia* was moved on to trans-Atlantic service. The peak, summer months, when that trans-ocean route was busy, the 615-foot long *Empress* sailed on a far Northern route—between Southampton and Quebec City. On these trips, however, her berthing arrangements were altered, reduced, and she carried the traditional trio of class-divided passengers: 387 in first class, 394 in tourist, and 358 in third. But in those cold, winter months, when Atlantic liner figures fell sharply and when the St Lawrence River froze over, she went cruising—often from New York—on two-, three-, and four-week jaunts around the sunny Caribbean Sea, but sometimes also on much longer, more expensive itineraries. Seventy days in 1935 and from one end of the Mediterranean to the other, for example, had a minimum cost of $600 or just a little more than $11 a day!

Cruising on the likes of the *Empress of Australia* was quite an extraordinary journey in the years between the wars. "We sailed at midnight—and thousands of people were at the New York pier to see us off. A British band in full uniform played on deck as we tossed streamers and cheered and cried," remembered Alice Keppel-Thomas. She was a passenger on a 1935 winter cruise aboard the *Empress of Australia*, a luxury cruise ship owned by the Canadian Pacific Company, the giant transportation combine. A 21,500-tonner, she had three tall stacks painted in golden yellow, carried about 500 passengers on these cruises, and had a superb reputation and loyal following

in her day. "Then, even the sailings were gala affairs," added Mrs Keppel-Thomas. "My whole family, sixteen in all, had come aboard and then squeezed into our stateroom. All of us drank champagne and ate canapes and little sandwiches off huge, crested, silver serving trays."

The late Mrs Keppel-Thomas was on a three-week West Indies cruise aboard the *Empress*. "We had 11 days of sea travel—leisurely and restful," she wrote in her journal:

> We'd have deck games in the morning, a big lunch in the columned dining room and then the whole ship napped from about 2 o'clock until 4. There wasn't a sound or even a knock on a stateroom door. Tea was next, a big event in itself. Men were in shirt, jacket and tie, ladies in day dresses and the waiters in immaculately starched jackets with polished brass buttons. While a string quartet played and the passengers danced, those waiters pushed trolleys and carried large trays laden with cakes and cookies and sandwiches.
>
> For dinner, we dressed in full evening clothes—long gowns and fur wraps and the main in tails. There were 14 formal nights altogether. As we dined, an orchestra played on a balcony. Afterward, there was dancing, sometimes a quiz, occasionally a film in the Main Lounge. But there really wasn't much to choose from. You enjoyed the ship itself, the sea, the far-off ports and lands, and those extraordinary star-filled tropic nights. The ship was usually "dark" by midnight.

"I never actually saw the *Empress of Australia*," said the late Everett Viez, a New York City-based travel agent in the 1930s. "But she was well known in Manhattan travel circles for her very spacious public rooms. She was also very popular for long cruises."

Another notation was added to the career several years later, in May 1939, of the *Empress of Australia*. Just months before the start of World War II, in May 1939, she crossed to Canada as something of a huge "royal yacht." Her primary passengers were Britain's King George VI and Queen Elizabeth, the parents of the future Queen Elizabeth II. It has been said that the *Empress of Australia* was selected at George VI's personal request.

After heroic duties in World War II, the now aged *Empress of Australia* remained in British Government service, carrying post-war servicemen and their families, and also ferrying immigrants out to Australia. A tired ship, she was scrapped in Scotland in 1952, just short of her fortieth birthday.

Bound for the east: The *Empress of Australia* outbound at Vancouver. (*Alex Duncan*)

Tea at four: First-class comfort. The Drawing Room aboard the *Empress of Australia*. (*Cronican-Arroyo collection*)

Above: The first-class smoking room on the *Empress of Australia.*
(*Cronican-Arroyo collection*)

Right: Five courses for dinner: The first-class dining room that was used
by King George VI and Queen Elizabeth during their May 1939 crossing.
(*Cronican-Arroyo collection*)

...ress of Australia, 1st Class Saloon, Buffet, etc.

Above left: An evening poster depicting the *Empress of Australia*. (*Norman Knebel collection*)

Above right: The trans-Atlantic services of Canadian Pacific. (*Les Streater collection*)

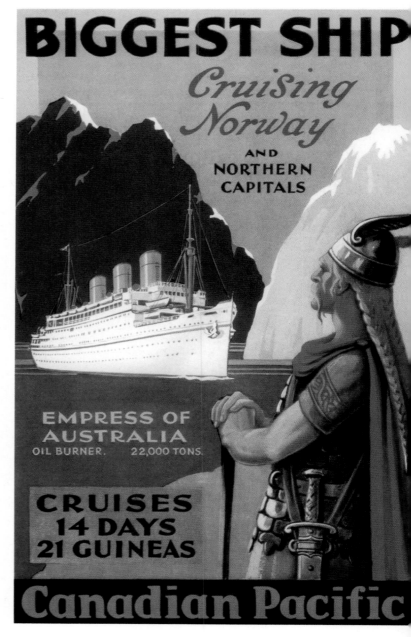

Above left: Canadian charm: The *Empress of Australia* below the Chateau Frontenac at Quebec City. (*Norman Knebel collection*)

Above right: Summer months: Cruising to the North Cape and Norwegian fjords. (*Les Streater collection*)

Above left: Mediterranean cruises as well. (*Les Streater collection*)

Above right: Political link: A connection of the then vast British Empire. (*Norman Knebel collection*)

Above: Dressed in flags: Outbound on a long cruise from New York on a winter's day in 1930. (*Cronican-Arroyo collection*)

Left: Together: The *Empress of Britain* (left) and the *Empress of Australia* at Southampton in May 1939. (*ALF collection*)

Left: Royal passengers: With King George VI and Queen Elizabeth onboard the *Empress of Australia,* departing on May 16, 1939. (*Cronican-Arroyo collection*)

Below: Rough seas on the North Atlantic with the royal couple onboard. This photo was taken from HMS *Repulse* on May 24, 1939. (*Cronican-Arroyo collection*)

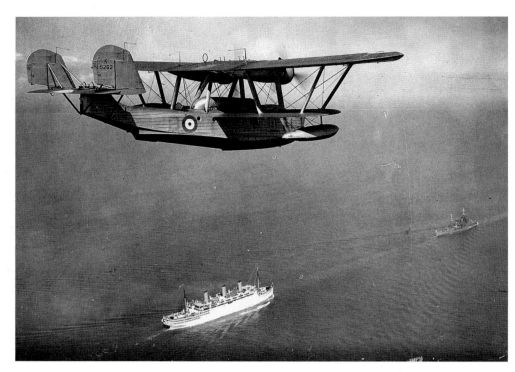

Left: Safety and security: The *Empress of Australia* on her royal crossing with RAF planes overhead. (*Cronican-Arroyo collection*)

Below: The *Empress of Australia* in Valletta harbor, Malta, in September 1945. (*Michael Cassar collection*)

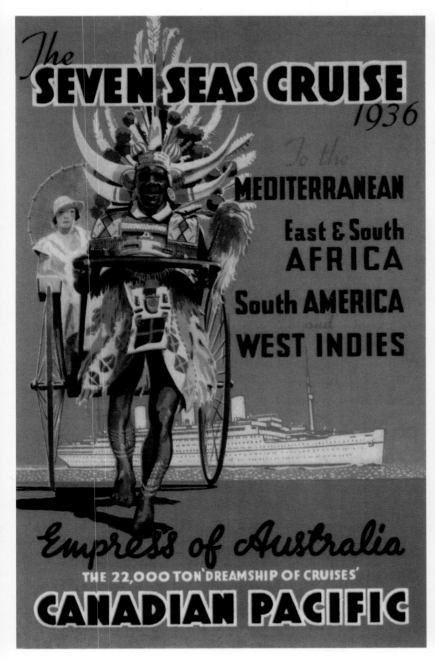

Above left: The aptly titled "Seven Seas Cruise" of 1936. (*Les Streater collection*)

Above right: Sailing to two continents: South America & Africa. (*Les Streater collection*)

The *Empress of Canada*

The fourth of the big Pacific liners for Canadian Pacific was an individual ship—she did not have a sister. She was a post-World War I creation, a ship created for a supposed boom in peacetime travel. Built by Fairfields at Govan, this 627-footer was launched on August 17, 1920 and would cost a much inflated £1.7 million. Indeed, Canadian Pacific's ship operation economics had changed from 1914. Alone, the *Empress of Canada* would have to earn as much as £60,000 more per voyage than the pre-war *Empress of Russia* and *Empress of Asia*. Shipboard expenses had gone up 350 percent by 1921, while fares had only increased by 185 percent.

With her completion delayed by shipyard and supplier strikes, the 21,517-ton *Empress of Canada* set off on her delivery voyage on May 5, 1922. She was routed from Falmouth to Hong Kong via the Suez. Manned by a crew of 530, she had accommodations for 488 first class, 106 second class, 288 third class, and 926 in Asiatic steerage.

Over the years, the 18-knot, twin-screw *Empress of Canada* had a number of notations. On September 1, 1923, she was at Yokohama when the Great Kanto Earthquake struck and she rendered rescue services. In January 1924, after being specially sent to New York, she offered Canadian Pacific's first around-the-world cruise. In March 1927, she collided with the Japanese passenger ship *Kinsho Maru* at Shanghai. In 1928, she was returned to her builders, Fairfields at Govan, to be re-engined and afterward made a round voyage between Southampton and Quebec City. After this, she sailed off to Panama, then to Vancouver, and resumed her Pacific sailings. Finally, in November 1932, she collided with another Japanese ship, the *Yetai Maru*, during a Kobe–Shanghai voyage.

Requisitioned for war service in November 1939 (following 200 Pacific crossings), the *Empress of Canada* became a trooper. She was soon off to ports around the world including taking part in the Spitzbergen Raid. Later dispatched to Southern waters, she departed from Durban on March 1, 1943 with 1,800 aboard, including 200 Poles released by the Russians following the Nazi invasion of their homeland, 400 Italian prisoners of war, and assorted naval personnel. Not sailing with a usual convoy, she took a roundabout course to go northward and, on March 12, was ordered to Takoradi to collect another 300 Italian prisoners. On March 13, however, the *Empress of Canada* was torpedoed off the West African coast and sank quickly—392 lives were lost. Those rescued were eventually brought to Freetown and later sent to the UK on Cunard's *Mauretania*.

Canadian Pacific's trans-Pacific service ended with the war, by 1940, and it was not resumed. It was felt—among other reasons—that trade to the Far East following the war would not be sufficient and that air travel (including Canadian Pacific Airlines) was firmly in the future. In 1945–46, Canadian Pacific thought briefly of restoring its Pacific service but then lost any further interest, considering the much-changed economic situation in Japan and the unstable political tone in China. The idea was quickly abandoned. Furthermore, only two liners from that pre-war service were still about. The surviving *Empress of Australia* became a fulltime trooper and then migrant ship, while the *Empress of Japan*, renamed *Empress of Scotland* in 1942, was restored for further duties, but as the Line's trans-Atlantic flagship.

Above: The handsome looking *Empress of Canada*. (*Cronican-Arroyo collection*)

Below: Another view of the classic three-funneled *Empress of Canada*. (*Cronican-Arroyo collection*)

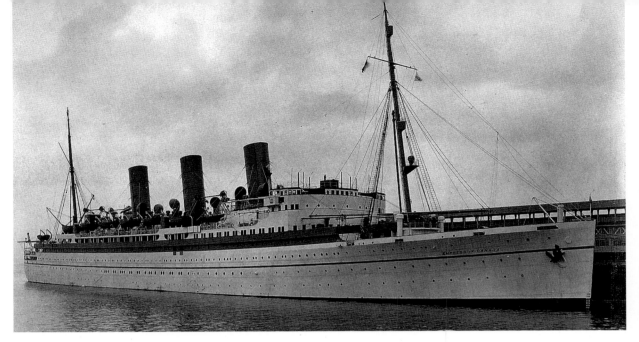

Above: The *Empress of Canada* repainted in white after 1927 and while berthed at Vancouver. (*Cronican-Arroyo collection*)

Left: The inviting Long Gallery aboard the *Empress of Canada*. (*Les Streater collection*)

Above: The *Aorangi* of the Union Line of New Zealand ran an affiliate service to Vancouver and Victoria but from Auckland and Wellington. (*Gillespie-Faber collection*)

Right: The enchanting Main Lounge aboard the *Empress of Canada*. (*Les Streater collection*)

2

SHIPS ON THE ATLANTIC

The *Scotian/Marglen*

Canadian Pacific had a sizeable fleet of Atlantic passenger ships in the 1920s, following the destruction and losses of World War I and with the resumption of busy normal passenger services. Immigration to Canada was especially significant and all while more economical cabin-class passages had become especially popular. Among the Canadian Pacific passenger ships of this period (1918–28), I have opted to list them in order of year of construction.

We begin with the 10,322-grt *Scotian,* a ship built by Harland & Wolff at Belfast in 1898. In her first life, she had been the *Statendam* of Holland America Line and used on the North Atlantic between Rotterdam, Channel ports, and New York. The Dutch sold her in 1911 to the British-flag Allan Line, who renamed the 515-foot-long ship *Scotian* for their Glasgow-Montreal service. She joined the war effort in August 1914, becoming a gray-painted troopship. Two years later, while still in military service, the 14-knot ship was transferred, along with the Allan Line fleet, to Canadian Pacific.

After the war ended in November 1918, she was quickly refitted for passenger service—carrying 304 in cabin class and 542 in third class—on the Canadian run in a joint Canadian Pacific-Anchor Line service from Glasgow and with westbound stops at Belfast. A further refit in 1922 saw her renamed as the *Marglen.* Afterward, and apart for a charter in 1925 for three Liverpool-Bombay voyages, her career was uneventful. Along with her increasing age, she was soon

redundant to Canadian Pacific's needs and so, in December 1927, was sold for £23,000 to Italian shipbreakers and then broken-up in the following year at Genoa.

The *Tunisian/Marburn*

Built by Alexander Stephen & Sons at Glasgow, the 10,576-grt *Tunisian* was commissioned in April 1900 for Allan Line's Liverpool-Halifax-Portland, Maine service. A 16-knot ship, she actually established a Canadian/trans-Atlantic record in 1903—six days and seven hours between Rimouski and Liverpool. As built, the 500-foot-long *Tunisian* could carry 240 in first class, 220 in second class, and 1,000 in third class.

Called to war duties in September 1914, the ship had a rather unusual assignment—she was at first used to house German POWs. Eventually, she returned to sea duties: trooping in the Mediterranean to the Dardanelles and out to the Middle East via Suez. She resumed austerity passenger service, making London-Montreal sailings, in 1919. A full refit followed a year later, with her quarters restyled for 310 in cabin class and 736 in third class. Soon back in normal passenger service, she was placed on the joint Canadian Pacific/Anchor Line service between Glasgow and Montreal and, in fact, introduced the first added call at Belfast in March 1922. Later that same year, as Canadian Pacific reorganized its "cabin class" services with ships with

SHIPS ON THE ATLANTIC 29

an "M" nomenclature, the *Tunisian* was renamed the *Marburn* and joining the *Marglen*, the *Marloch*, the *Marvale*, and others.

But ships such as the twenty-seven-year-old *Marglen* were tired and worn out by 1927. She was soon laid-up off Southend with little possibility of much further service. She did in fact make one final passenger crossing (with emigrants), from Antwerp to St John's, Newfoundland, in April 1928. That September, she was sold to Italian shipbreakers and later broken-up at Genoa.

The *Victorian/Marloch*

The 10,645-grt *Marloch*, while built by Workman, Clark & Company at Belfast in 1905, did not enter actual Canadian Pacific service until December 1921. The 520-foot-long ship had begun her career as the *Victorian* for the Allan Line. While moderately sized and certainly not overly luxurious, she and her sister, the *Virginian*, were noted as the very first steam turbine and first triple screw liners on the Atlantic. Built for 18-knot service speed, the *Victorian* actually achieved 19 ½ knots on her sea trials.

Used on Allan Line's Liverpool–Montreal run (or to Saint John, New Brunswick, in winter), the *Victorian* was requisitioned by the British Admiralty for war duties beginning in September 1914. She began by serving as a fully outfitted armed merchant cruiser. During the subsequent war years, the management of the ship changed to Canadian Pacific and then, in July 1917, full transfer was completed. She was not, however, released from military services when the war ended in November 1918, but kept on for further trooping services. She was still in full use in as late as 1920–21, ferrying troops between the UK and colonial India.

Finally returned to Canadian Pacific in December 1921 and then fully refitted by Fairfields at Glasgow, she was converted from coal to oil burning, given new steam turbines, had her service speed reduced to 14 knots, and her passenger quarters reduced as an "intermediate liner." She was categorized as a "cabin class liner" and offered lower fares to passengers. She returned to Liverpool–Montreal service in December 1922 as the renamed *Marloch*, but her Canadian Pacific days ahead were rather limited. Aside from ramming and sinking the British steamer *Whimbrel* off Flushing in Holland in 1924, she had a rather quiet, undistinguished life. Beginning in 1925, she was

often laid-up, used mostly as a relief to other passenger ships during their overhauls and refits. This provided less and less use, however, and in April 1929, she was sold for demolition. Her end came in the hands of Thomas W. Ward Shipbreakers at the Pembroke Dock in South Wales.

The *Corsican/Marvale*

Another Allan liner was the 1907-built *Corsican*, built by Barclay, Curle & Company at Glasgow for Liverpool–Canada services. Used as a troopship during World War I (including long voyages to and from India and a transfer to Canadian Pacific), she was used to repatriate Canadian troops in 1918–19 and then did austerity passenger service. She was more fully converted and upgraded for full passenger service in 1922 and became the *Marvale*. Her days were numbered too, however. On May 21, 1923, during a voyage from Quebec City to Glasgow, she was caught in a thick fog, went aground, and was wrecked on Freel Rock, Cape Pine, Newfoundland. Fortunately, all passengers and crew were saved.

The *Empress of Scotland*

Briefly, in 1906–07, she ranked as the largest ship afloat, but that record soon passed to Cunard's brilliant, 32,000-ton *Mauretania*. Constructed by Vulcan Werke AG at Stettin, this 24,500-tonner was intended to be the *Europa* for Hamburg America Line's Hamburg–Southampton–Cherbourg–New York service. She was, with some modifications, a development of another big Hamburg America liner, the *Amerika*. Naming plans changed, however—the 677-foot-long ship was launched by the Empress of Germany as the *Kaiserin Auguste Victoria*. After entering North Atlantic service in May 1906, she was in fact somewhat less successful than intended—she became known as a "slow, hesitant roller."

Laid-up at Hamburg beginning in August 1914 and throughout World War I, she was taken at war's end by the British and considered reparations. Moved to Hull (in 1919) and used for a time for troop accommodation, she was soon chartered to the United States Shipping Board to carry returning American troops from Europe to

Above: With four masts, the *Empress of Scotland* was the company's largest Atlantic liner in the 1920s. (*Cronican-Arroyo collection*)

Right: Crossing to the historic North Atlantic. (*Les Streater collection*)

Opposite left: The cover for a passenger list. (*Les Streater collection*)

Opposite right: The *Empress of Scotland* to the Med, departing February 1925. (*Les Streater collection*)

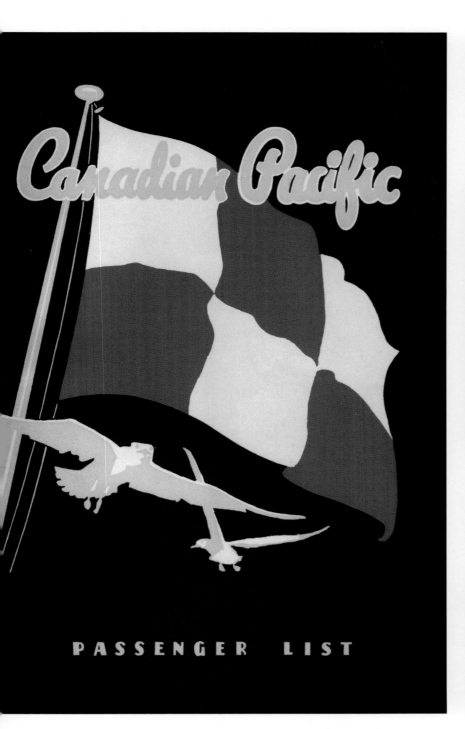

Above: Tragic destruction: The *Empress of Scotland* burning on December 10, 1930. (*Author's collection*)

Left: Canadian Pacific offered a diverse group of mostly wintertime cruises. (*Les Streater collection*)

Opposite left: Another Mediterranean cruise. (*Norman Knebel collection*)

Opposite right: There were calls at as many as forty ports during a world cruise. (*Les Streater collection*)

New York. A year later, she was chartered again, this time to Cunard, to run some Liverpool–New York crossings. She sailed as a Cunard liner, but under the name *Kaiserin Auguste Victoria*.

Further changes were ahead: the *Kaiserin Auguste Victoria* was officially allocated as reparations to Canadian Pacific in May 1921, and she was promptly renamed *Empress of Scotland*. Instead of going to a British yard for a thorough refit, however, she was returned to her German builders at their Hamburg yard for a major refit. Converted to oil burning, her passenger quarters were restyled—459 in first class, 478 second class, and 536 third class. Her tonnage was now relisted as 25,037, making her Canadian Pacific's largest liner.

Freshly painted and dressed in flags, the *Empress of Scotland* entered Canadian Pacific service in January 1922 with a special Southampton–New York crossing. Once there, she was off, on charter to a New York travel agency, on a two-month cruise around the Mediterranean. She called at over twenty-five ports during that long, luxurious voyage. Later, in the spring, she sailed to Quebec City (she could not go to Montreal) to begin regular service to and from Southampton. A popular ship, she had the notation of carrying the Prince of Wales (later Edward VIII and then the Duke of Windsor) and his entourage following a Canadian tour. Among many royal passengers over the years on Canadian Pacific liners, the Prince crossed from Quebec City to Southampton.

The *Empress of Scotland* was an early victim of the Great Depression. After Wall Street crashed in October 1929 and the worldwide depression began, passenger traffic began a steady decline. It had dropped in fact by as much as 50 percent in five years by 1935. In December 1930, the liner was withdrawn from service and promptly sold to shipbreakers—Hughes, Bolckow, at Blyth—but her ending was rather troubled. While at the breakers, on December 10, she caught fire, was gutted, and then, overloaded with firefighters' water, sank at her berth. Raised five months later, there was still more trouble—she broke in two while being moved at the shipbreakers.

The *Empress of Britain* (1905)/*Montroyal*

According to prolific author Duncan Haws, this ship and her sister (the ill-fated *Empress of Ireland*) were to have been the *Empress of Austria* and *Empress of Germany*. Such names were evidently aimed at appealing to the lucrative German and East European westbound migrant trade. Launched on November 11, 1905, however, as the *Empress of Britain*, the first ship went on to become one of Canadian Pacific's more successful ships (the ill-fated *Empress of Ireland* sank in the St Lawrence River in 1914).

Built by Fairfields at Glasgow, this 14,200-ton twin-stacker was designed with accommodation for nearly 1,500 passengers—310 in first class, 350 in second class, and 800 in third—and she had a crew of 250. Fitted with quadruple expansion engines, she was listed with a service speed of 18 knots. Following her maiden crossing, in May 1906, she quickly established a record: five days and twelve hours between Father Point and Liverpool. Later, she did even better, cutting her own record to five days and eight hours.

Used as an armed merchant cruiser beginning in August 1914, she soon proved impractical in such a role, however, and so was converted for trooping. Although damaged in a fire while moored in the River Mersey in October 1915, her further war service was accident-free. In 1919, after being returned to Canadian Pacific and running some austerity crossings, she was fully refitted and improved later that same year. Afterward, she was a more efficient oil-burning ship. Quite efficient, in fact, she could run a Liverpool–Quebec City–Liverpool round voyage in fifteen days.

After being allocated to "cabin class" category in 1924, her quarters were rearranged for 600 in cabin class and 800 in third class. Assigned to further Liverpool service (and later from Antwerp, Southampton and Cherbourg), she was renamed the *Montroyal*.

No longer efficient, however, by 1929, she was laid up and then offered for sale. In the following summer, she found her way to quite unusual shipbreakers at Stavanger in Norway. Her ballroom was removed, however, before the final demolition and placed in the Sola Strand Hotel. Thoughtfully, it was named the Montroyal Ballroom.

In camouflage coloring, the *Empress of Britain* arriving at New York's Chelsea Piers during World War I. (*Author's collection*)

Above: Simple yet classic design: The *Marglen* in the 1920s. (*Alex Duncan*)

Left: An evocative sunset view of the *Empress of France*, the former *Alsatian* of Allan Line. (*Norman Knebel collection*)

Opposite left: Arrival in cosmopolitan Montreal. (*Norman Knebel collection*)

Opposite right: 1920s travel on Canadian Pacific's *Empress of France*. (*Norman Knebel collection*)

CANADIAN PACIFIC
TO CANADA & UNITED STATES

FOR PARTICULARS AS TO FARES, &c.,

APPLY WITHIN

Montreal
and Jacques Cartier Bridge

James Crockart

TRAVEL
Canadian Pacific

C.P.O.S.
TO
CANADA
&
UNITED STATES

Above left: An early Allan Line sailing schedule. (*Norman Knebel collection*)

Above right: Very affordable third-class fares—$15 in third class. (*Norman Knebel collection*)

The *Empress of China/Empress of India/ Montlaurier/Monteith/Montnairn*

Built at Tecklenborg in Germany, this ship was commissioned in June 1908 as North German Lloyd's *Prinz Friedrich Wilhelm*. A 17,300-ton ship, she was created for the then-booming North Atlantic trade, especially the westbound migrant trade. As built, the 590-foot-long ship could carry 425 in first class, 338 in second class, and 1,756 in third class. She was used in Bremerhaven–Southampton–Cherbourg– New York service. It was during one of these crossings that she sent out an ice report, on April 12, 1912, which had it been acted upon two days later would have saved the ill-fated *Titanic*.

On a summer cruise to Norway, on August 2, 1914, just as World War I had started, the ship tried to return to Germany, but then grounded and had to take refuge in the small port of Odda. A second attempt to return to German waters two years later also ended in trouble—she went aground off Denmark. Later salvaged, she finally sailed for home waters and was kept at Kiel.

Ceded to Britain after the war ended, in 1919, she was reactivated to carry American soldiers home to New York. A year later, she was used by the Canadian Government to carry more soldiers home and even made one long voyage from Bombay to Halifax. In 1921, she was bought outright from the Reparations Commission by Canadian Pacific, and in August, she was promptly renamed the *Empress of China*. But that name did not last long: within two months, by October, she was renamed the *Empress of India*. She was refitted, but kept largely as a reserve ship—filling-in during refits and overhauls of other company ships. She made some Liverpool–Canada crossings, but also charter troop voyages to the Mediterranean for the British Government. But in little more than a year, in December 1923, she was renamed once again, becoming the *Montlaurier* and joining the "M" class of cabin-class liners. Yet there were further name changes ahead. In June 1925, she was renamed the *Monteith*, but was again renamed in little more than a month as the *Montnairn*. Again, she was a "fill-in" ship, which included running occasional Antwerp–Quebec City migrant sailings. After reaching Southampton in October 1928, she was laid-up, being moored off Netley for over a year. In December 1929, she was sold to Italian ship breakers and sailed to Genoa for demolition.

The *Alsatian/Empress of France*

She and her sister, the *Calgarian* (torpedoed and sunk in 1918), were the largest and finest liners built for the Allan Line, which was absorbed by Canadian Pacific in 1916. An especially fine-looking liner with twin funnels and twin masts, she was completed on the eve of World War I, being delivered by her builders, William Beardmore & Sons of Glasgow, in December 1913. She was designed for over 1,600 passengers in three classes for the Liverpool–Montreal run (to Halifax and Saint John, New Brunswick, in winter). She had but a short stint in commercial service, however. Within nine months, in September 1914, she was requisitioned for use as an armed merchant cruiser. On her patrol duties, she covered 266,000 miles, examined 15,000 ships, and escorted numerous Atlantic convoys.

After being decommissioned from war duties in December 1918, she was promptly reconditioned, upgraded, and renamed the *Empress of France*. Soon, back in regular service, she quickly set a record— Liverpool to Quebec City in five days and twenty-three hours. In winter, she was sent to New York for cruising, to the Caribbean, and, under charter to a Manhattan-based tour company, on a luxurious, four-month circumnavigation of the globe. So popular, the second world cruise was operated by Canadian Pacific itself rather than on a charter. On the Atlantic, she was quite successful and on one occasion had the Prince of Wales as one of her passengers, although listed under an alias and so, as he said, "he might join in the shipboard fun."

Converted to oil burning (in 1924) and with extended service that often included Hamburg, the 571-foot-long *Empress of France* was shifted to the Pacific in the fall of 1928 for a year on the Vancouver-Far East run, but by late 1929, she was back on the North Atlantic as well as in seasonal New York cruise service. However, numbers on her crossings were rapidly dropping following the start of the Great Depression. Little time was wasted to implement company cuts, and the *Empress of France* was laid-up in the Clyde in October 1931. She remained at her moorings for three years, until October 1934, when she was sold off for £35,000 to scrappers W. H. Arnott Young. She was towed to Dalmuir on November 24 and the demolition quickly began.

  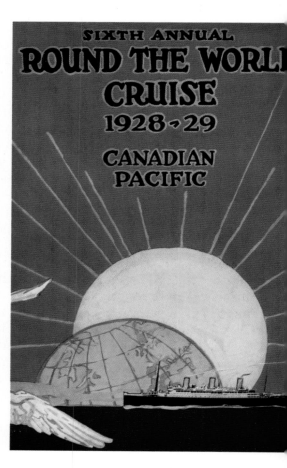

Above left: Fun at sea: Cruising on Canadian Pacific. (*Les Streater collection*)

Above middle: Patriotic travel: Come cruising on British ships! (*Les Streater collection*)

Above right: Another long, luxurious world cruise. (*Les Streater collection*)

Opposite above: The classic-looking *Montroyal*. (*Alex Duncan*)

Opposite below: The *Montnairn*. (*Alex Duncan*)

The *Metagama*

One of two sisters (the other being the *Missanabie*, sunk in September 1918), the 12,242-grt *Metagama* was a very practical ship, built primarily for the low-fare and migrant trades. Launched at Barclay Curle's Glasgow yard in November 1914, several months after World War I started. Built to carry 520 cabin and 1,138 third-class passengers, she was pressed into regular service, however, rather than on war duties. Beginning in March 1915, she ran regular voyages between Liverpool and Saint John, New Brunswick. On the eastbound voyages, troops occupied the third-class quarters.

The 520-foot-long liner was reconditioned after the war. She resumed Atlantic crossings and eventually finished on the Antwerp–Southampton–Cherbourg–Quebec City–Montreal route, but she too was an early victim of the Great Depression. By 1930, the *Metagama* was laid-up and never resumed sailing. Almost four years later, in April 1934, she was sold to scrappers at Bo'ness in Scotland.

The *Melita & Minnedosa*

Laid down in 1914 at Barclay Curle's Glasgow plant, these 14,000-ton sister ships were initially intended for the Hamburg America Line, but the war changed those plans and instead, being set aside and incomplete for three years, they were towed to Belfast in 1917 for completion. The first ship was launched as the *Melita* and was quickly in service between Liverpool and Eastern Canada. Her voyages were later extended to Antwerp and Southampton. Quarters were arranged for 490 in cabin class and 1,300 in tourist (later, in 1926, changed to 206 cabin class, 545 tourist, and 588 third). Also used for low-fare cruising, but then was laid-up as well, the *Melita* was sold to Italian scrappers in June 1935. However, after being towed to Genoa, the ship was resold to Italian Government for use in Mussolini's Abyssinian War. Renamed the *Liguria*, the 546-foot-long ship was placed under the management of the Italian Line, but then later shifted to Lloyd Triestino and repainted with a white hull and all-yellow funnels.

The *Liguria* (ex-*Melita*) was a casualty of World War II. First, while in use as an Axis troopship, she was damaged off Tobruk in July 1940, and months later, on January 22, she was set on fire and sunk—also at Tobruk. Her remains were not salvaged for nine years, until 1950, and the wreckage was towed to Savona, Italy, for scrapping.

The career of the *Minnedosa* was quite similar to that of her sister. She was delayed owing to World War I, completed in 1918, and then used in Canadian Pacific austerity service between Liverpool and Quebec City. However, once in regular service, she had her troubles: she was rammed at her Antwerp berth in 1924 and damaged in a shipyard fire at Newcastle a year later. Once the Great Depression set in, she was, like her sister, struggling. The *Minnedosa* was laid-up at Glasgow in 1931 and then sold off four years later to the Italians for scrapping, similar to her sister. Before the scrapping could commence, she was resold to the Italian Government, assigned to the Italian Line, and later Lloyd Triestino and renamed the *Piemonte*. She too was then used as a troopship in the Abyssinian War.

The war years were not fortunate to the former *Minnedosa* as well. She was torpedoed and badly damaged near Messina in November 1942. Later, while lying in Messina, she was hit several times by Allied bombers. She sank on May 4, 1943, resting on her starboard side in shallow harbor waters. The wreckage was finally raised in the spring of 1949 and was later towed to La Spezia for scrapping.

Above: The *Montclare* passing under the Forth Bridge bound for Rosyth. (*Cronican-Arroyo collection*)

Below: The *Montcalm* dressed in flags and during a cruise. (*Alex Duncan*)

Another view of the *Montcalm*. (*Author's collection*)

Another view of the *Montcalm*, but during a cruise. (*Michael Cassar*)

The *Montclare* at sea. (*Author's collection*)

Above: The *Montrose* during a cruise. (*Alex Duncan*)

Below The *Montclare*. (*Les Streater collection*)

CANADIAN PACIFIC S.S. MONTCLARE.   CABIN CARD ROOM.

CANADIAN PACIFIC S.S. MONTCLARE.   CABIN. "THE SHOP."

Above: The Card Room aboard the *Montclare*. (*Author's collection*)

Right: The gift shop on the *Montclare*. (*Author's collection*)

Opposite above: The Main Lounge on the *Montclare*. (*Author's collection*)

Opposite below: The Smoking Room. (*Author's collection*)

CANADIAN PACIFIC S.S. MONTCLARE.   CABIN LOUNGE.

CANADIAN PACIFIC S.S. MONTCLARE.   CABIN SMOKE ROOM.

The cozy Writing Room. (*Author's collection*)

Simpler in style: The third-class lounge aboard the *Montclare*. (*Author's collection*)

The *Montcalm, Montrose, & Montclare*

Optimistically planning for greater post-World War I traffic on the North Atlantic, but with more moderate-sized, "cabin class" style ships, Canadian Pacific planned five and possibly six of this *Montcalm*-class of 16,500-tonners. Only three were actually built, however.

Measuring 546 feet in length and with accommodations for 1,810 passengers (542 in cabin class and 1,268 in low-fare third class), they were each manned by a crew of 390. The cabin-class quarters were improved over Canadian Pacific's other "cabin class" liners using the "M" nomenclature. The *Montcalm*, built by John Brown at Clydebank and completed in December 1921, had steam turbine engines, which rendered a service speed of 17½ knots. These ships initially ran on the Liverpool–Canada run, but later sailed on the Hamburg/Antwerp–Southampton–Cherbourg–Canada service. They were refitted and improved in 1926 and the berthing arrangements changed a year later to three classes.

With the Great Depression greatly cutting into Canadian Pacific's North Atlantic liner operations, the *Montcalm* turned to bargain cruising, often for as little as £1 per day, beginning in 1932 and usually from Liverpool to the likes of Spain, Portugal & the Atlantic Isles, the Mediterranean, and, in summer, to the Norwegian fjords and the Northern Cities (Oslo, Stockholm, Copenhagen, etc.).

The *Montcalm* soldiered on through the 1930s before—with the start of World War II in September 1939—becoming the armed merchant cruiser *Wolfe*. Yet further changes were ahead: in 1941, she became a troopship and then, after being sold outright to the British Admiralty, a submarine (and later destroyer) depot ship a year later. She survived the war, but only to be laid-up in 1950 and then sold to breakers at Faslane in late 1952.

The *Montrose*, laid down as the *Montmorency*, had a very similar history. Completed in May 1922, she plied the North Atlantic until, in 1932, she began fulltime bargain cruising. Once the war began in September 1939, she too was called to duty, becoming the armed merchant cruiser *Forfar*. The former *Montrose* did not survive the war, however; she was torpedoed and sunk by a German U-boat off Ireland on December 2, 1940.

Completed in August 1922, the third and last of this trio was to have been named the *Metapedia*, but was completed as the *Montclare*. After trans-Atlantic duties in the '20s, she too spent much of the '30s in low-cost cruising. She became an armed merchant cruiser in the late summer of 1939 and then, in 1942, was converted to a submarine depot ship before being sold to the Admiralty. Decommissioned and laid-up in 1955, she was delivered to breakers at Inverkeithing on February 3, 1958.

3

STURDY SHIPS: FOUR DUCHESSES

Above: Dressed in flags: The *Duchess of Richmond* on another winter cruise. (*Alex Duncan*)

Right: A view of the *Duchess of Bedford*. (*Les Streater collection*)

Opposite: The handsome *Duchess of Atholl* during a cruise. (*Author's collection*)

Left: The *Duchess of Richmond* arriving at Lisbon. (*Les Streater collection*)

Below: Deck games on the *Duchess of Richmond*. (*Author's collection*)

Entrance Hall and Elevators on a Duchess of the Atlantic

Lounge on a Duchess of the Atlantic

The spacious Foyer of a "Mont" steamship

Above left: Comfort at sea: Cabin-class interiors aboard the *Duchess* liners. (*Norman Knebel collection*)

Above right: Further interior views of the *Duchess* liners. (*Norman Knebel collection*)

The *Duchess of Bedford* at Valletta, Malta, in a photo dated May 14, 1946. (*Michael Cassar collection*)

Another view of the *Duchess of Bedford* in wartime colors. (*Les Streater collection*)

Above: The *Duchess of Atholl* at war. (*Les Streater collection*)

Right: Post-war and restoration: A striking view of the outbound *Empress of Canada* at Montreal. (*Canadian Pacific Steamships*)

Opposite: Dressed in flags, the *Empress of Canada* arrives in Montreal on her post-war maiden crossing. (*Cronican-Arroyo collection*)

Right: Destruction: The burned-out, capsized *Empress of Canada* at Liverpool in January 1953. The *Empress of France* is just behind. (*Gillespie-Faber collection*)

Left: The sad sight of the capsized *Empress of Canada*. (*Author's collection*)

Below: Righted, but cut down and minus its superstructure, the remains of the *Empress of Canada* will soon be towed away to the scrappers. (*Author's collection*)

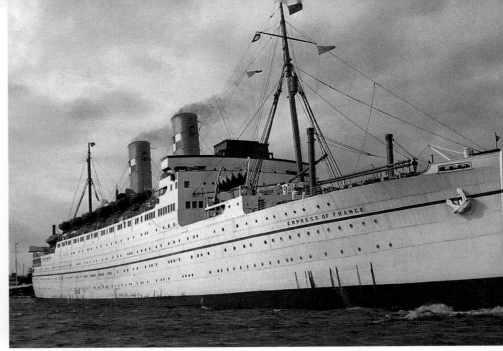

Above left: The *Empress of France* arriving at Montreal. (*Canadian Pacific Steamships*)

Above right: The *Empress of France* seen at the Princes Landing Stage, Liverpool. (*Canadian Pacific Steamships*)

Below: The *Empress of France* in the River Mersey. (*Canadian Pacific Steamships*)

The *Duchess of Bedford*

While certainly not as large or, to some, as important as Cunard and White Star on the North Atlantic, Canadian Pacific Steamships—as part of the huge Canadian Pacific Railways Company—certainly produced its share of important, often quite notable passenger ships. The company began in Great Lakes passenger shipping in 1864 and then gradually diversified into coastal, trans-Atlantic and trans-Pacific services. In 1921, arms were consolidated as Canadian Pacific Steamships Ltd, part of the world's largest transport combine. The name endured until 1968 when it was, in a "new age" of business and corporate advertising, renamed CP Ships. Amid the changes, the company's famed red and white checkered flag (dating from 1891) disappeared as well. The company moved into containerized freight shipping, eventually became part of Canada Maritime, and was finally bought out (for $2 billion) by the German conglomerate TUI AG, which planned to merge it with its Hapag-Lloyd division. The integration was completed in August 2006 and CP Ships, as well as the maritime legacy of Canadian Pacific, passed into history.

By the late '20s, there was a quartet of twin-stackers, four Duchesses—the *Duchess of Bedford*, the *Duchess of Atholl*, the *Duchess of Richmond*, and the *Duchess of York*—that were noted Canadian Pacific passenger ships. They were, however, also known to be often unsteady at sea and so dubbed "the Drunken Duchesses." Handsome, if conservative-looking ships, with twin masts and those twin funnels, they were created by what was then one of Britain's and the world's best known and most respected shipbuilders, John Brown & Company Limited of Clydebank in Scotland.

The 600-foot-long *Duchess of Atholl* was to be the first of this quartet, two of which would later be important parts of Canadian Pacific's renewed, revived post-World War II fleet. While under construction, there was an accident with one of the new ship's turbines, however, and so the second sister, the *Duchess of Bedford*, was moved to front position. Her construction schedule was actually advanced so that she could make the advertised first sailing of these "Duchess liners," on June 1, 1928. The 20,022-grt ship had been launched just months before, on January 24, and named by Mrs Stanley Baldwin, wife of the then Prime Minister. She was completed with accommodations for 1,570 passengers—580 in cabin class, 480

in tourist class, and 510 in third class. The London-registered ship had a crew of 510. Driven by steam turbines, the twin-screw *Duchess* soon established a record—Liverpool to Montreal in six days, nine hours, and thirty minutes—and cut nearly a full day off the previous record. Designed to make 17½ knots, she could manage 18 knots and, for periods, could make as much as 20 knots. Canadian Pacific was delighted with her.

Very quickly and beginning in 1930–31, the worldwide depression affected the new *Duchess* and her sisters. Trans-Atlantic travel dropped considerably and so the *Duchess* ships were often sent off on cruises—and occasionally even skipped posted Canadian Pacific voyages and were temporarily laid-up at Liverpool. Canadian Pacific were actually quite happy, however, to lease the *Duchess of Bedford* to the Furness-Bermuda Line in the winter of 1933, for use on the New York–Bermuda run, making six-day roundtrips until their new *Queen of Bermuda* was ready to enter service that February.

The *Duchess of Bedford* made news on May 8, 1933—there was a rumor that she had struck an iceberg off Newfoundland, was sinking, and, along with her passengers and crew, had 500,000 pounds of gold bullion onboard. The rumor persisted until the following day, when the ship radioed that all was well and continuing her voyage. Two months later, on July 13, however, she did indeed hit an iceberg in the Belle Isle Strait between Newfoundland and Labrador. There were no damages or injuries. The only other notation in the 1930s seems to be her rescue of thirty-two French seamen in June 1939 from a barquentine, which sank after striking an iceberg off Newfoundland.

The *Duchess of Bedford* was called to military service soon after Britain entered World War II in September 1939. She was now painted overall in gray and used as a high-capacity troopship in worldwide operation. Happily, she was a lucky ship as well. She was anchored in the Mersey during the ten-day Blitz on Liverpool but managed to escape any damages. She was of course a prime target, but soon was ordered to the Clyde for safety. Later, she delivered 4,000 Indian troops and forty nurses to Singapore just days before the Japanese invasion in January 1942. Fortunately, she then got away just five days before the actual surrender, carrying a large group of refugees including 875 women and children. She then returned to the North Atlantic and delivered the first US troops—673 officers and 6,507 men—to be landed at Liverpool. Soon afterward, she sank an enemy submarine (and while using a World War I gun mounted on her stern), damaged another sub, and then later, in 1942, was herself stranded during the French North African operations. Eventually, she was towed free by two passenger ships also far from home waters: the Irish Sea packets *Ulster Monarch* and *Royal Ulsterman*.

After repairs, the *Duchess of Bedford* was soon back to war duties, serving in the Sicilian and then the Italian landings. In fact, in 1943, she was the very first troop transport at the Salerno landings. Near the war's end, in the spring of 1945, she carried a large number of Russians to Odessa in the Black Sea. They had been liberated by the advancing Allied armies, and then she returned with an equally large number of Allied prisoners that had been rescued by the Soviet forces. By the war's end in August 1945, the *Duchess of Bedford* was valiant, but a worn, rusted, and certainly tired ship. She certainly had a fine record—she carried 231,000 troops and covered 350,000 miles in six years of war service.

Another two years of military duties followed; post-war, she carried returning troops as well as war brides and children westbound to Canada. Finally, she was released and happily returned to Canadian Pacific. While British shipyards were crammed and sometimes waitlisted with refit as well as construction work in 1946–47, the *Duchess of Bedford* found a spot—she was sent to the big Fairfield Shipbuilding & Engineering Company yard at Govan for reconditioning for peacetime service. She was modernized, upgraded, repainted with an all-white hull, and was to become the *Empress of India*, but Indian independence (in August 1947) changed the appropriateness of that naming and so instead she was rechristened *Empress of France*. Her quarters were now reduced and made two-class, for a maximum of 700 passengers: 400 in first class and 300 in tourist class. Her machinery was thoroughly overhauled, and even new propellers were fitted. With her twin funnels now painted in buff and the Company's checkered house flag painted on each side, she resumed Liverpool–Montreal sailings on September 1, 1948. In winter, when the St Lawrence River was ice-clogged, the *Empress* turned around at St John, New Brunswick, where passengers made rail connections to and from Montreal.

"There is a good deal in a ship's name," wrote passenger appraiser of the late 1940s and '50s C. M. Squarey in his book *The Patient Talks*. He wrote of the *Empress of France* in August 1949:

There's instantaneous appeal in the imperial name *Empress of France*. But having been given an imposing name, it is necessary [for a ship] to be imposing—and, in one word, this is precisely what this ship is. There is an air of certainty about her, the certainty that she will disembark you as a delighted customer, a confidence about her that she can, and will, really please you.

There are two things that I noticed. Firstly, there is no first class Smoking Room, but the former Smoking Room now being called the "Empress Room" and designed and used mainly for entertainment purposes. The second was flowers. How seldom does one see floral decorations in a dining saloon or a bowl of flowers in a lounge arranged with anything that starts to approach the "Constance Spry" touch? This ship does.

The *Empress of France* was selected for a great honor in October 1951: she was to carry Princess Elizabeth and the Duke of Edinburgh across the Atlantic on their North American tour. Renewed and serious concerns about the health of King George VI, the Princess's father, caused the tour to be delayed, however. Instead, the royal couple consequently flew to Canada (but later returned as planned onboard the *Empress of Scotland*).

The *Empress of France* was a very popular ship, and a ship with a "soul." Many crewmembers, for example, and while rotating between the other *Empress* liners, preferred to return to her. Others declined transfers from her altogether.

During her winter refit of 1958–59, the thirty-year-old *Empress of France* was slightly modernized. Her funnels were tapered to give her a more modern appearance. However, time was running out—the commercial jet appeared for the first time in October 1958 and the competition proved unbeatable. Shipping lines began losing business, and quite quickly; furthermore, with the brand-new *Empress of Canada* due to enter in the spring of 1961, the aged *Empress of France* was soon redundant. Her final crossing was scheduled for October 1960. Two months later, on 19 December, she left Liverpool for the breakers at Newport in nearby Monmouthshire. Just three days before, another well-known Atlantic liner, Cunard's *Britannic*, left Liverpool for the breakers at Inverkeithing. The Atlantic liner trade had begun its gradual, but definite decline.

During the demolition, some of the ship's wood paneling was removed and sold for use in the White Hart Pub in Machen, near

Caerphilly, South Wales. It endured for decades, but the pub was closed in the spring of 2016. It was reported that the pub was up for sale and would most likely be demolished to make way for a small housing development. The paneling will most likely be lost in the demolition.

The *Duchess of Atholl*

Launched by the *Duchess of Atholl*, this 20,119-grt ship was delayed during construction and so became the second sister rather than the first. Her career seems to be uneventful other than losing her rudder during a December 1935 crossing and arriving three days later at Liverpool. Her screws were used for steering. Called to war duties as a troopship in December 1939, she was part of a large convoy in May 1942 that took part in the Madagascar landings. Six other liners (the *Oronsay*, the *Sobieski*, the *Winchester Castle*, the *Karanja*, the *Keren*, and the *Atlantis*), along with twenty-seven warships were involved. Later that same year, on October 10, the *Duchess of Atholl* was torpedoed by a German U-boat when at sea and 200 miles north of Ascension Island. Four ships were lost.

The *Duchess of Richmond*

Restored after war service, the *Empress of Canada* was actually the first of the post-war *Empress* liners to resume commercial service on the Atlantic. The 20,325-grt ship sailed from Liverpool on July 16, 1947, bound for Montreal. Canadian Pacific had returned to the passenger ship business.

Also a product of the John Brown shipyard at Clydebank, the *Empress of Canada* was launched on June 18, 1928, but as the *Duchess of Richmond*. Her maiden voyage, beginning on January 26, 1929 was actually a six-week cruise from Liverpool to the Atlantic Isles and West Coast of Africa. While her capacity was specially reduced to under 600 for cruising, she was designed to accommodate up to 1,590 passengers—580 in cabin class, 480 in tourist class, and 510 in third class.

After that maiden cruise, the *Duchess of Richmond* was placed in Atlantic passenger service, making winter season crossings to St

John, New Brunswick. She was soon in the news, however, having grounded in fog off St John on April 28, being delayed and with her passengers transferred to another company liner, the *Montcalm*. In November 1932, she collided in fog off Sorel, Quebec, with a Cunard liner, the *Alaunia*. In 1935, she made more pleasant news: she carried the newly married Duke and Duchess of Kent off on their honeymoon cruise. The Duke was the son of King George V and Queen Mary; his wife was the popular Princess Marina.

Two more incidents followed for the *Duchess of Richmond*. While on a cruise, she was in a collision at Gibraltar on December 18, 1935. It meant an extended stay for repairs, with her 748 passengers missing their Christmas at home. Eighteen months later, in April 1937, during a pilgrims' cruise to the Holy Land, she broke away from her moorings in a full gale while at Haifa. Her 1,000 passengers were stranded ashore until the gale subsided.

After World War II started in September 1939, the *Duchess of Richmond* made evacuation crossings to Canada until the winter of 1940, when she was officially called to duty as a troopship. Her first voyage was Liverpool to Suez with troops. Her wartime career, while useful, was uneventful. During the invasion of North Africa, she was quite close to the P&O liner *Strathallan* when that ship was sunk by two torpedoes on December 21, 1942. Near the end of the conflict, in March 1945, the *Duchess of Richmond* carried 3,700 Russian POWs from France to Odessa. Eight months later, in November, she brought the last prisoners from Sumatra and Singapore home to Liverpool. Her final military voyage, in March 1946, was from Bombay to Liverpool, and upon arrival, she was held in the Mersey until four smallpox cases were removed and placed in isolation. At the same time, the *Georgic* arrived at Liverpool with one known case. Precaution was necessary such that some 10,000 people aboard the two liner-troopships took part in a massive vaccination, the largest ever undertaken at Liverpool.

The *Duchess of Richmond* was refitted for her return to passenger service, beginning in May 1946, by the Fairfield shipyard at Govan. Repainted in all-white and with the company's new funnel colors, she was renamed *Empress of Canada*. Her passenger quarters had been restyled, modernized, and greatly reduced—to 397 in first class and 303 in tourist class. Beginning in the summer of 1947, she handled Canadian Pacific's Atlantic liner service singlehandedly, making sailings every three weeks in each direction.

The *Empress of Canada*'s post-war days were all too short, however. The year 1953 was to be a boom year for Atlantic traffic because of the coronation of Queen Elizabeth II in London that June. Canadian Pacific's ships were heavily booked, often to capacity, on most sailings. Some travelers were on wait lists. In preparation, on January 10, 1953, the *Empress of Canada* entered Liverpool's Gladstone Dock for a month-long winter overhaul. Her next sailing was posted for February 11, but disaster struck; on an otherwise quiet Sunday, January 25, at 3.30 p.m. and while lying in No. 1 Branch Dock, a fire broke out. The first discovery of fire aboard the otherwise quiet liner was not made until forty minutes later. The fire was actually first observed by a worker on a nearby floating grain elevator, who hailed the *Empress* just across the dock, but no notice was taken at first. It was a most unfortunate and, in ways, unnecessary tragedy. Firefighters from all over North West England were called as the liner soon burned furiously. Then tons of water was poured on the ship such that she soon capsized, turning on her port side and became a burnt-out hulk lying on its side. She was a complete loss. Quickly, needing a replacement ship, Canadian Pacific bought French Line's *De Grasse* and had her in trans-Atlantic service by spring as the renamed *Empress of Australia*.

Work on salvaging the gutted, capsized *Empress of Canada* began almost immediately. She was, after all, occupying a very important berth at Liverpool. It was an enormous task, one very similar to the salvage of the far larger *Normandie* at New York in 1942–43, however. That great French liner had also caught fire, capsized, had to be partly scrapped, and finally righted and towed away to the scrappers. First, the masts, funnels, and then the superstructure of the *Empress of Canada* had to be cut away. She was, of course, beyond repair, and she would never see service again. Over a year passed before, on March 6, 1954, the salvage was completed. It was in fact the greatest salvage operation of its kind ever tackled in Europe.

The salvage job had been given to a French company and was very complicated. Some locals were used in the operation, including one man whose task was to feed cables underneath the hull. He used a fire hose to make a path through the mud underneath the ship and then pulled through a rope, which was then used to pull progressively larger wires. As he went under the 600-foot-long ship, he recalled that the mud would seal up behind him, so he had to keep moving forward. It was said to be a "horrible job," and several divers were later killed in the process.

The hull of the *Empress of Canada* was up-righted by a combined system of parbuckling and buoyancy. The project was paid for by the Mersey Docks & Harbour Board, who pledged £380,000 to cover the costs. Eventually, sixteen hawsers made the pull and the *Empress* began moving—and almost with great ease. Six pontoons, each filled with 104 tons of water, pulled down on the exposed starboard side while eleven other pontoons, filled during the night with compressed air, pushed upwards on the submerged port side. The wreck moved silently and quickly toward a point of balance. It actually took only thirteen minutes to come from 88 degrees to 44 degrees.

There was an added problem for the ship, however. Unexpected by the salvagers, the ship had slid 20 feet along the mud bottom of the Gladstone Dock. The blocks on the winches had come together and complicated the righting of the ship. Finally, adjustments were needed before the *Empress* righted itself. In a total of only fifty-five minutes, the ship was sitting on the mud and at an angle of only 9 degrees. The deadweight pulls needed to right the liner had been 15,000 tons. She was patched along the port side and then fully righted, a process that lasted another ten weeks. The hulk was taken to the Gladstone Graving Dock on June 30, over five months since the fire. Very carefully, she was moved by a team of four Alexandra Towing Company tugs and all while drawing nearly 41 feet, which gave her a very delicate clearance of only 2 feet over the entrance sill into the graving dock.

The blackened, rusted hulk of the *Empress of Canada* was sold in the summer of 1954 to Italian scrappers for £130,000. The two propellers were removed and then sold separately, for a combined £8,000. Altogether, the salvage had cost the Mersey Docks & Harbor Board £466,000. The hulk departed from Liverpool on September 1, 1954, under the care of the 836-ton, deep-sea tug *Zwarte Zee*. Once at La Spezia in Italy, the hulk would be scrapped in nine to ten months and her steel fed into Italian recycling mills.

Apart from the crew aboard the tug itself, twelve Dutch seamen sailed aboard the *Empress*. Quarters had been specially built in the hulk, near the former Empress Room in first class, and included sleeping spaces, a coal galley stove, toilet and shower facilities, and a motor-driven dynamo for lighting. It was projected that, at a speed of 5 knots and dependent on weather, the tow to Italy would take three to six weeks. The towing gear included wire cables and manila ropes

However, there were continued problems for the *Empress of Canada*. After rounding the Skerries, the *Zwarte Zee* ran into a full gale. Just off Tuskar Rock, the towlines parted, leaving the ship adrift for some time. Once the lines were reattached, the plan was to take the hulk into Dublin Bay and then, according to plans, to Belfast for further repairs. Plans changed, however, and instead the tug and its charge proceeded to the Clyde. Later, once back at sea, more gales were encountered and there were further delays. Forty days after leaving the Mersey, the hulk of the *Empress of Canada* finally reached La Spezia on October 10. By mid-1955, she was scrapped completely.

The Court of Inquiry investigation into the cause of the fire was concluded two months after the fire, in March 1954. The cause was a discarded, lighted cigarette in a B-deck cabin. Fire precautions for idle ships in port were, of course, much reduced compared to those when operating, with crew and passengers for the *Empress*.

The *Duchess of York*

The last of the class, the *Duchess of York*, which was to have been named *Duchess of Cornwall*, was torpedoed off the Moroccan coast on July 11, 1943, eleven of her complement were lost and then her burning wreckage was later deliberately sunk by Allied warships.

The last of the four *Duchess* quartet was named on September 9, 1928 by HRH the Duchess of York, who later became Queen Elizabeth and then Queen Elizabeth The Queen Mother. Used in North Atlantic service, the *Duchess of York* was used by the Furness-Bermuda Line between January and May 1931 on the six-night New York–Bermuda cruise run.

Requisitioned for trooping in the winter of 1940, she was soon off on a voyage to Canada with 500 German POWs, 1,700 captured German seamen, and 400 internees. The voyage was expectedly tense and a near riot occurred resulting in the death of one sailor.

4

SPEED QUEEN OF THE PACIFIC

The *Empress of Japan*

"They had the finest fleet on the Pacific back in the 1920s—with their fine *Empress* liners: *Empress of Australia, Empress of Asia, Empress of Russia,* and *Empress of Canada,*" recalled the late Everett Viez, an ardent ship enthusiast, traveler and onetime New York City-based travel agent.

> They offered a superb, exacting, multi-class service between Vancouver and Victoria and the Orient—to Honolulu, Yokohama, Kobe, Nagasaki, Shanghai, Hong Kong and Manila. The high spirits and increasing passenger loads of the second half of the '20s prompted a decision to build the biggest, best and fastest Canadian Pacific liner for Vancouver service. She went on to become one of the finest passenger ships of the twentieth century.

The 666-foot-long *Empress of Japan* was built by one of the great shipbuilders of the day: Fairfield Shipbuilding & Engineering Co. Ltd of Glasgow. She was completed in the spring of 1930. Designed to be the fastest and most luxurious liner yet on the Vancouver–Far East service, she was bestowed with a regal sounding name, honoring Imperial Japan. Emerging as a handsome ship, the new *Empress* was, in fact, a refined, slightly smaller version of the giant *Empress of Britain*, which was then still being built, quite nearby, at the John Brown yard at Clydebank. The Pacific liner had a slightly more "relaxed" profile with three evenly slanted funnels (the third was in fact a dummy). The big *Empress of Britain* was more imposing, mighty, even more majestic.

The *Empress of Japan* was richly appointed. Her decor strongly reflected the recent moderne, a style later dubbed Art Deco. It was not extreme, however, and did not preclude warmth and a sense of comfort. The public areas were made more pleasing to the eye as well as inviting by added touches: scattered soft chairs and long sofas, silk pillows, area carpets on highly polished floors, potted palms, stylized columns. The berthing was arranged in Pacific style: 399 in first class, 164 in second class, 100 third class, and 510 in so-called Asiatic steerage (primarily for Asian migrants going eastward to Canada).

After completing an introductory Atlantic crossing to the St Lawrence, she then set sail—in the summer of 1930—for Hong Kong via the Suez Canal. Arriving in Vancouver for the first time that August, she averaged a very respectable 21 knots on her first Pacific passage. In the following spring, on a run between Yokohama and Victoria, she averaged 22.27 knots. No ship on the Pacific could outpace her, and her record stood for thirty years, until the 1960s, when it was surpassed by an American freighter, the *Washington Mail.*

A sample sailing from Vancouver and Victoria outbound for Honolulu, Yokohama, Kobe, Nagasaki, Shanghai, Hong Kong, and Manila in May–June 1937 read:

Outbound at Vancouver, the very handsome *Empress of Japan*. (*ALF collection*)

Left: Great maritime power: The fastest liner on the Pacific in the 1930s. (*Alex Duncan*)

Opposite: Shipboard comfort: The first-class gallery on the *Empress of Japan*. (*Canadian Pacific Steamships*)

Cha-cha lessons: The spacious Ballroom. (*Canadian Pacific Steamships*)

Above: Trans-Pacific on the *Empress of Japan*. (*Les Streater collection*)

Left: The splendid indoor swimming pool. (*Canadian Pacific Steamships*)

Above left: Fastest route on the Pacific. (*Les Streater collection*)

Above right: The glorious White Empresses of the Pacific. (*Les Streater collection*)

Above left: The great Pacific *Empress* liners. (*Les Streater collection*)

Above right: Maritime contrast: The *Empress of Japan* arriving in Hong Kong. (*Les Streater collection*)

Promoting the link between Vancouver, Victoria, and Honolulu. (*Norman Knebel collection*)

Empress of Russia	May 1
Empress of Japan	May 15
Empress of Asia	May 29
Empress of Canada	Jun 12
Empress of Russia	Jun 26

And a sample for a *Empress of Japan* voyage, also 1937:

Vancouver/Victoria	May 15
Honolulu	May 20
Yokohama	May 29
Kobe	May 30
Shanghai	Jun 1
Hong Kong	Jun 4
Manila	Jun 6

Following the outbreak of war in September 1939, Canadian Pacific's trans-Pacific service was suspended and their liners called to duty and scattered. The *Empress of Japan*, painted over in grays, was designated as a troopship and sent to the South Pacific to take part in at least two noted convoys. The first, in January 1940, included three columns of converted troopers: HMS *Kent* led the *Empress of Japan*, the *Empress of Canada*, the *Orcades*, and the *Rangitata*; the battleship HMS *Ramillies* led the *Orion*, the *Orcades*, and the *Dunera*; and then the French warship *Suffren* led the *Strathaird*, the *Strathnaver*, the *Otranto*, and the *Sobieski*. In the following May, the *Empress of Japan* was part of one of the biggest convoys of the war, one that included the *Queen Mary*, the *Aquitania*, the *Empress of Britain*, the *Mauretania*, the *Andes*, and the *Empress of Canada*. The combined tonnages of these seven liners was over 277,000.

In October 1942, prompted by Japan's entry into the war, the *Empress of Japan* was given special government permission to be renamed, becoming the *Empress of Scotland*. Ships could not be renamed during the war, primarily for security reasons. Later used on the North Atlantic troop shuttle, she was not decommissioned and returned to Canadian Pacific until the fall of 1948. She had steamed over 500,000 miles during eight years of military service, made three around-the-world trips, and carried over 200,000 personnel. Refitted at her builders at Glasgow, she was styled for trans-Atlantic service—between Liverpool and Quebec City.

The refitted *Empress* now wore red-and-white chequers on her three funnels and had greatly reduced berthing figures—458 in first class and 205 in tourist class. She joined two other pre-war liners, the *Empress of Canada* and the *Empress of France*, in providing weekly service in each direction. Fares aboard the *Empress of Scotland* were from $246 in first class and $156 in tourist class.

Her most distinguished passengers came aboard in November 1951. She carried HRH Princess Elizabeth and the Duke of Edinburgh and their party home from a highly successful North American tour (and similar to the one in May–June 1939 carried out by the Princess's parents, King George VI and Queen Elizabeth, who crossed both ways by sea—the *Empress of Australia* over, the *Empress of Britain* on the return). Princess Mary, the Princess Royal, and Princess Alice, the Countless of Athlone, were among other royals that used Canadian Pacific liners during their travels. Princess Elizabeth and Prince Philip boarded from a specially arranged stop at Portugal Cove in Newfoundland and then disembarked six days later at Liverpool. The voyage was said to have some "very rough patches"—the Princess, it was later reported, did not miss a meal while the Duke, himself a naval officer, took to his bedroom at times. The royal train was waiting at Liverpool and then delivered the royal couple to London. Sadly, within two months, King George VI would be dead and the young princess would become Queen Elizabeth II.

In winter, the *Empress of Scotland* crossed to New York each December and then began three or four months of cruising to the sunny Caribbean. She then became an all-first class ship and had a portable pool fitted to her aft deck.

With the addition of the brand-new *Empress of Britain* and the *Empress of England* in 1956–57, the *Empress of Scotland* was made redundant to Canadian Pacific's requirements by the fall of 1957. Together with the *Queen Mary*, they were by then the Atlantic last three-stackers (a third liner with three funnels, the *Queen of Bermuda*, was on the New York–Bermuda run). Laid-up at Liverpool, the *Empress of Scotland* was twenty-eight years old and might well have gone to the breakers, but good fortune prevailed. She was sold for £1 million to the West Germans, to the newly formed Hamburg Atlantic Line. Provisionally renamed the *Scotland*, she was sent off to Hamburg.

Left: Post-war: The *Empress of Scotland*, still in military service, in the harbor of Valletta, Malta, in 1948. (*Michael Cassar collection*)

Below: Following her post-war refit, the *Empress of Scotland* on sea trials in 1950. (*Canadian Pacific Steamships*)

Right: The *Empress of Scotland* at Liverpool. (*David Williams collection*)

Below: Outbound on a winter's morning from New York, bound for the warm waters of the Caribbean. (*Gillespie-Faber collection*)

Left: Blustery skies silhouette the handsome *Empress*. (*Author's collection*)

Below: The first-class Main Lounge in the 1950s. (*Richard Faber collection*)

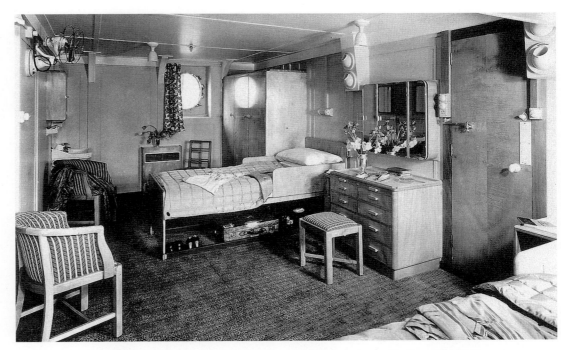

A first-class double-bedded cabin in the 1950s. (*Richard Faber collection*)

The first-class cocktail lounge. (*Richard Faber collection*)

Shipbuilding and Shipping Record, February 20, 1964

Above left: Turning the three-funnel *Empress of Scotland* into the twin-funnel *Hanseatic*. (*Author's collection*)

Above right: Repairs at Hamburg, 1961. (*Author's collection*)

Left: German style and service: The *Hanseatic* departing New York in 1961. (*Author's collection*)

Berthed at Madeira during a cruise, the *Hanseatic* on the left; the *Statendam* to the right. (*ALF collection*)

Above: Afternoon arrival at New York's Pier 97 with the *Queen Frederica* to the far right. (*Port Authority of New York & New Jersey*)

Below left: Farewell: Outbound on the River Elbe. (*Author's collection*)

Below right: The fire will prove to be destructive and decisive for the former *Empress of Japan*. (*Author's collection*)

Flames: Ablaze at New York in September 1966. (*Author's collection*)

Gutted and largely rebuilt and modernized, the former *Empress* was all but unrecognizable when she appeared on the Atlantic liner scene as the streamlined, twin-funnel *Hanseatic* in the following July. The passenger accommodation had been greatly enlarged—eighty-five in club-like, upper-deck first class and 1,167 in very comfortable tourist class. Better standards also prevailed—90 percent of all tourist cabins had a private toilet and shower. Used in trans-ocean service between Cuxhaven (Hamburg), Southampton, Cherbourg, and New York, she attracted considerable attention as reviving West Germany's largest liner to date (the 32,200-grt *Bremen*, also rebuilt having been the former French *Pasteur* in her first life, surpassed her a year later, in July 1959). The *Hanseatic*'s actual tonnage increased from 26,313 to 30,029 and—with the addition of a new bow—her length from 666 to 672 feet.

During the winter months and increasingly throughout the year, especially after the first jet flights began in October 1958 and Atlantic liner services began their long, but steady decline, the *Hanseatic* turned to cruising. Her itineraries were diverse: from New York to Bermuda, Nassau, and the Caribbean; from Port Everglades (Fort Lauderdale) to the Caribbean; from Cuxhaven on summer trips to the North Cape and Baltic, and in winter to Madeira and the Canaries; and on steadily popular fly-sail cruises from Genoa around the Mediterranean and out to West Africa.

Her end was untimely, however. While loading passengers at New York's Pier 84, on September 7, 1966, she caught fire. Smoke poured out over the river from windows, portholes, and ventilators. Firefighters poured water onto the burning ship, but were especially cautious. They did not want to repeat the *Normandie* fire and have the ship overloaded with water and capsize. With her sailing to Europe canceled and her passengers sent over instead to the likes of the nearby *Queen Mary*, the scorched *Hanseatic* was later towed over to the Todd shipyard in Brooklyn's Eire Basin for inspection and possible preliminary repairs. But the stench of smoke had permeated throughout much of the thirty-six-year-old ship and so any thought of repairs were abandoned. Within weeks, on October 10, she was towed to Hamburg and delivered to local scrappers. Some fittings were removed first, such as deck chairs, which were sent over to the *Homeric* of the affiliate Home Lines. Hamburg Atlantic itself was revived, but as the German Atlantic Line, using the former Israeli *Shalom*, which, in 1968, became the "new" *Hanseatic*.

5

THE GREATEST & GRANDEST EMPRESS

The *Empress of Britain*

The French added the stunning *Île de France* in 1927, then the Germans—in almost extraordinary revival from the ruins of World War I—added not one but two super liners, the *Bremen* and the *Europa* in 1929–30. Then, on the drawing boards, there was also two big liners for the Italians and, largest of all, super ships for Cunard, White Star, and the French Line (the White Star ship would be cancelled, however). Even after the Wall Street Crash in October 1929, the start of the worldwide depression and with a 50 percent slump in trans-Atlantic passenger traffic beginning, there were some delays, but little else seemed to change. Spirits and therefore future projections for new liners, some of the most lavish yet, were high. Among others, Canadian Pacific—based on the high spirits and optimism of the late '20s—looked forward.

The great Canadian Pacific Company was at its peak and had the prestigious distinction of "spanning the world"—trans-Atlantic by liner from Britain to Eastern Canada, across North America by rail, and then a second fleet of liners on the Pacific that went from Vancouver to the Orient. The beautiful, white-hulled *Empress* liners were perhaps at the lead in this vast organization and operation. The Pacific service had just been topped by the aforementioned *Empress of Japan*, a 26,000-tonner commissioned in 1930. She was one of the finest liners on the Pacific and also the fastest.

But then a look to the North Atlantic. Canadian Pacific also planned a second liner, even bigger, and more lavish than the *Empress of Japan*. She was the 42,000-ton *Empress of Britain*. The 748-foot-long ship was built by renowned John Brown shipyard on the Clyde and was launched on June 11, 1930, after being named by the then very popular Prince of Wales (who later became Edward VIII and then the Duke of Windsor). There was added distinction to the occasion: for the first time in history, launch proceedings were broadcast throughout the British Empire and, rather expectedly, to Canada and the United States.

From her royal launching, this liner generated almost extraordinary interest. One journalist wrote of her: "She was like no ordinary ship, but a bold Canadian bid for a topmost seat in the sun of shipping supremacy." On her maiden voyage, Viscount Rothermere, proprietor of the *London Daily Mail*, had "no hesitation in describing her as the finest vessel ever launched." Even after the far larger *Queen Mary* appeared in 1936, the *Empress of Britain* was still regarded by many as the most luxurious ship afloat.

Carrying comparatively few passengers (1,195—465 in first class, 260 in tourist, and 470 third class), the new *Empress* was Britain's biggest liner in almost twenty years, since the *Aquitania* of 1914. Her long, white hull was doubly strengthened for ice (for nine months of the year, she would ply the North Atlantic between Southampton, Cherbourg, and Quebec City). She had five holds as well: three for general cargo, the fourth for insulated goods, and the last for passenger baggage. On the outside, her designers opted for unusually mammoth funnels, which were in deep contrast to her

Empress of Britain, in service 1931, of 40,000 tons gross register, 24 knots speed—a de luxe flyer of the seas to make the Atlantic crossing in five days—a steamship that will set new standards of luxurious ocean travel.

Above: An early rendering of the *Empress of Britain. (Norman Knebel collection)*

Right: A travel agent model of the superb *Empress of Britain. (Cronican-Arroyo collection)*

Above: Waterborne: In the Clyde. (*Author's collection*)

Right: Installing the great funnels at John Brown's yard. (*Canadian Pacific Steamships*)

Leaving the John Brown yard. (*Author's collection*)

Onboard the splendid *Empress of Britain*: The first-class foyer. (*Canadian Pacific Steamships*)

Cocktails at six: The splendid Cathay Lounge. (*Author's collection*)

The first-class cocktail lounge. (*Author's collection*)

The magnificent indoor pool. (*Author's collection*)

Above: The vast, upper sports deck. (*Author's collection*)

Right: Bon voyage! The thunderous whistles sound. (*Canadian Pacific Steamships*)

Opposite: The Ballroom. (*Author's collection*)

owners' initial desire for more normal-sized ones. Together with a well-balanced, almost orderly superstructure, the three giant stacks added considerably to overall senses of size, power, and security. In daylight, she presented a most handsome form and great ocean liner style, and altogether unquestionably ranked as one of the great liners of the 1930s; at night, with her buff funnels floodlit, her appearance became even more dramatic and imposing.

Her 758-foot-long hull was capped by a balanced superstructure capped by three enormous funnels. "I remember seeing the *Empress of Britain* docked at Pier 61, at the foot of West 21st Street, in Manhattan. My first view was on a winter's night and those three funnels were floodlit. They looked like gas tanks. They were overwhelmingly big, but they worked on the *Empress*. They added to her great appeal as a true luxury liner. In every way, she was one of the greatest ships of her time," recalled John Gillespie, who, as a boy, lived just blocks away from that 21st Street pier and the visiting liners.

Her innards were, in a word, sumptuous. There was the columned, traditional Mayfair Lounge, which could be contrasted against the angular, stunningly modern, very Art Deco Cathay Lounge. The Salle Jacques was ranked as one of the finest shipboard restaurants while the Empress Ballroom and The Mall became established shipboard spaces. There was a large indoor pool, a gymnasium and a full squash court located on the highest deck, between the funnels.

"She was the most gorgeous ship. She was probably the most luxurious world cruise ship of all time," recalled Everett Viez.

Her Mayfair Lounge was extremely beautiful and the Cocktail Lounge delightful. She had more cabins with private facilities than any other ship then doing long cruises. She was intended for this dual-purpose from the start. She was purposely designed for luxury cruising. Actually, I think, in the end, she was better known for her cruises than her crossings. Externally, I felt she did have a top-heavy look. Those stacks were too large. But it all worked. And she was so symmetrical. Her cruiser stern was another attractive feature.

The *Empress* was built from the start with the added intention of spending each winter as a cruise ship and, more specifically, as a world cruise ship. Each January, she would leave New York's Chelsea Piers, with her outer propellers specially removed to reduce drag and save fuel, for as long as 140 days—for the Mediterranean, Suez, India, the Dutch East Indies, Hong Kong, China, Japan, and then homeward across the Pacific to Hawaii, California, and the Panama Canal before making a springtime return to Manhattan. Her capacity for these cruises, which became standard for 1930s luxury travel, was reduced from 1,195 to 700 all-first class. She became more club-like. Considering her size, she offered passengers an unparalleled amount of space per passenger.

A sample Atlantic sailing schedule from Montreal (or from Quebec City only for the *Empress of Britain* and *Empress of Australia*) in May–June 1937 and highlighted by the Coronation of George VI in London read:

Duchess of Bedford	May 8
Duchess of Richmond	May 14
Montclare	May 15
Empress of Britain	May 15
Duchess of York	May 21
Montcalm	May 26
Duchess of Atholl	May 28
Empress of Australia	May 29
Duchess of Bedford	Jun 4
Montclare	Jun 5
Duchess of Richmond	Jun 11
Empress of Britain	Jun 12
Empress of Australia	Jun 16
Duchess of York	Jun 18
Duchess of Atholl	Jun 25
Empress of Britain	Jun 28

In 1938, the *Empress of Britain* set off on another long, winter world cruise, but with a difference. Avoiding the Far East because of the growing conflict between Japan and China, she would call at Australia for the first time. Australian maritime historian Alf Batchelder wrote of the ship's first visit to Melbourne: "The City had never seen anything quite like the 1938 visit of the *Empress of Britain*. For anticipation, interest and sheer excitement, not even the memorable 1978 maiden visit of the *Queen Elizabeth 2* could match it."

As early as September 1937, it was already rumored that the "largest ship ever to make a complete circumnavigation of the globe" might

Above left: At Southampton with a flying boat in the foreground. (*ALF collection*)

Above right: The great Atlantic fleet of Canadian Pacific. (*Les Streater collection*)

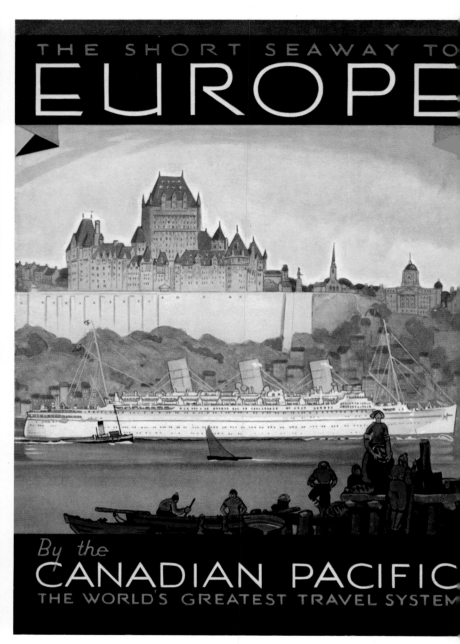

Above left: Sun & fun: Healthy living onboard Canadian Pacific. (*Norman Knebel collection*)

Above right: Canadian waters: The mighty *Empress of Britain*. (*Les Streater collection*)

Another view at Southampton. (*Author's collection*)

Out of the water: Looking tall and mighty, the *Empress of Britain* in the big floating dock at Southampton. (*Author's collection*)

Above: World cruising: Passing under San Francisco's Golden Gate Bridge. (*Canadian Pacific Steamships*)

Right: Repairs: In the big King George V Graving Dock at Southampton. (*Author's collection*)

Opposite: Festivity: Her maiden call at Melbourne, Australia, April 1938. (*Anton Logvinenko*)

World cruising: A visit to Wellington, New Zealand, 1938. (*ALF collection*)

TRANSITING THE PANAMA CANAL

Transiting the Panama Canal. (*Author's collection*)

The *Empress of Britain* arriving at Wellington, New Zealand. (*Canadian Pacific Steamships*)

visit Melbourne as well as Sydney. Soon after, there was a suggestion that the even larger, 51,700-ton *Bremen* might visit Australian waters, but this never came to pass. The Australian Government was further delighted with the news that the *Franconia* of Cunard and Hamburg America's *Reliance* would be rerouted and visit Australia. These calls were seen as opportunities of popularizing Australia and perhaps encouraging further visits. There were even "dreams" of a growing Australian cruise industry as 200 well-to-do Australians booked passage on the *Empress of Britain* (and with another sixty boarding in New Zealand) for remainder of the cruise.

There was even more excitement when it was revealed that the *Empress of Britain* along with the *Reliance* would be arriving at the same time, April 5–6, 1938. There was a rush for applications for visitor passes for the *Empress of Britain* and Melbourne's City Motor Service specially laid on fifteen new Studebaker limousines for use by the ship's passengers. Even Canadian Pacific's general manager of their cruise department was sent to Australia to ensure all went well with the visit. Newspapers prepared advance announcements and preliminary articles about the *Empress of Britain*'s visit. They noted that she was twice the size of liners that regularly visited, ships such as the *Mariposa*, the *Strathmore* and the *Orcades*. The port of Melbourne required special dredging and permission had to be given for the ship to make a nighttime departure. The harbor had to be cleared for the big *Empress* and special warning signals and lights put in place.

Closer to the liner's arrival, the Melbourne newspapers spoke of the wealth and opulence of the ship, its voyage, and its passengers. For the 300 world cruise passengers, their combined wealth was placed at £10 million. Each of them had at least an annual income of £5,000 and this was compared to £200 annual income of a typical Australian worker. The imaginations of many readers were all but staggered. Still later, it was revealed that the wealthiest passenger was Sir Montague Burton, a tailoring magnate with a fortune put at £4 million. He was followed by Alexander Maclean, whose pharmaceutical and toothpaste empire put his worth at £3 million. Other notables aboard included Arthur Loew, the vice-president of Metro Goldwyn Mayer; Mr A. Klaveness, managing director of Norway's Klaveness shipping group; and Prince Andrew of Greece, the father of the future Duke of Edinburgh.

The liner arrived in Sydney on April 2, as the city was celebrating its sesquicentenary celebrations. The ship made a majestic entrance into harbor, surrounded by ferries and pleasure craft, and used six tugs to berth at Woolloomooloo. Brilliantly lighted, she departed on April 4 to a band send-off, waving crowds, and more craft in attendance. Her next stop was Melbourne for another triumphant visit. That visit to Australia of the *Empress of Britain* was a great occasion.

The *Empress of Britain* made further headlines and featured in newsreels when she brought King George VI and Queen Elizabeth (later the Queen Mother) home from their highly successful, friendship-building North American tour in 1939. The royal couple had crossed to Canada weeks before, but on another Canadian Pacific liner, the *Empress of Australia*. Dowager Queen Mary and the little princesses, Elizabeth (later HM the Queen) and Margaret, greeted their parents upon arrival at Southampton. However glamorous and exciting this was, and added to the ship's other distinctions, she was not a great financial success. With her services to and from the St Lawrence, the *Empress of Britain* failed to build a strong, even an added following among Canada-routed passengers. Instead, most travelers still preferred the New York route. Those long world cruises were victims of both the on-going depression and simply the vast, added expense of running such luxurious jaunts.

In 2016, I met eighty-five-year-old Jack Harding from Liverpool. He told me of his link to Canadian Pacific and the *Empress of Britain*:

My uncle served on the *Empress of Britain*. He was a first-class waiter. He was very proud. On those world cruises, he saw the world: India, China, the Suez & Panama Canals. He'd come home and was the 'star' of the family with tales and presents from faraway places like Bombay and Shanghai and San Francisco. And he was among the staff that sailed aboard the *Empress of Britain* when it carried King George VI and Queen Elizabeth home from Canada and back to England [June 1939]. That was a big event, the conclusion of an important visit that renewed friendship and stirred goodwill and loyalty with Canada and especially America. The trip was a big success, including the King & Queen meeting with President Roosevelt, which would be an important bond in the years ahead, when World War II began and Britain needed American support. My uncle was lined with other crew when Queen Mary, Princess Elizabeth and little Princess Margaret came aboard in Southampton Water to welcome home the King and the Queen. Later, during the war, my uncle served on the *Empress of Australia*, which was then carrying troops all over the world. Then he

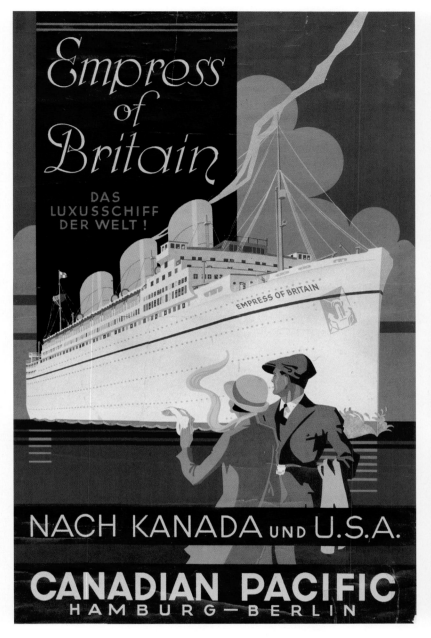

Above left: Promotion to German travelers. (*Norman Knebel collection*)

Above right: "The most spacious big liner afloat" according to Canadian Pacific publicists. (*Norman Knebel collection*)

Sailing from San Pedro, California. (*Author's collection*)

Chance meeting: The *Empress of Japan* (left) and *Empress of Britain* (right) meet at Manila. (*Les Streater collection*)

"THE EMPRESS OF BRITAIN READY TO LEAVE SOUTHAMPTON DOCKS FOR CANA

SOUTHAMPTON DOCKS
THE GATEWAY TO THE WORL
Owned and Managed by the Southern Railwa

Above: Visit and use the Southampton Docks. (*Author's collection*)

Left: The striking aerial view: Maiden departure from Southampton. (*Les Streater collection*)

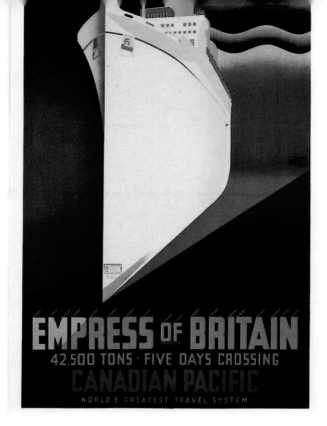

Left: Striking, Deco-style poster art. (*Norman Knebel collection*)

Below: A squadron of RAF flying boats hover over the *Empress of Britain* as she arrives in the Solent, on June 22, 1939, with King George VI and Queen Elizabeth aboard. (*Cronican-Arroyo collection*)

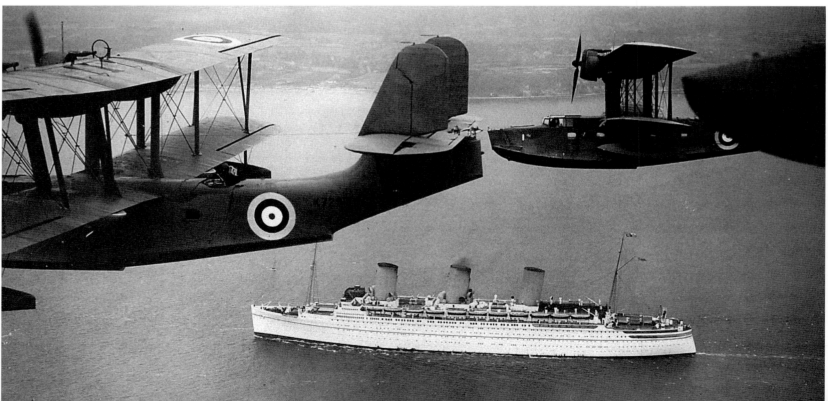

Above: Resting between voyages at Southampton. (*Author's collection*)

Right: The *Empress of Britain* arriving at Southampton in a view dated May 5, 1938. (*Cronican-Arroyo collection*)

Arriving at Southampton,
1939. (*Cronican-Arroyo
collection*)

The *Empress of Britain* on the left with the *Olympic* behind and the *Berengaria* on the right. (*Author's collection*)

Tropic mood: Passing through the Panama Canal. (*Author's collection*)

Above: The glorious *Empress of Britain*. (*Author's collection*)

Left: Sailing from San Pedro, California. (*Author's collection*)

THE GREATEST & GRANDEST EMPRESS   109

left the sea just after the war ended, in 1946. He had about three years ashore, but deeply missed the sea. It was in his blood. He just loved life at sea and, of course, the travel. He joined Cunard in Liverpool and, because of his experience aboard the famous *Empress of Britain*, he was assigned immediately to the new *Caronia*. That ship was soon said to be the most luxurious cruise liner in the world and it too cruised everywhere. My uncle especially liked the *Caronia*'s long world cruises. He'd be gone for five or six months, leaving England in January and not returning until May or June. He actually died at sea, onboard the *Caronia*, in 1959, of a sudden heart attack. It seemed somehow fitting: He died while the ship was on one of those long world cruises, in the Red Sea. Fittingly, he was buried at sea.

The *Empress* left Southampton on September 2, 1939, the day after the peace-breaking invasion of Poland. She had far more passengers aboard than normal. Evacuees and frightened, often desperate tourists without actual cabin accommodation were assigned to cots set-up in the public rooms and even in a special arrangement up in the squash court. Once at Quebec City, she was temporarily laid-up, pending further decision by the Admiralty. Two months later, in November, she was formally called to duty. Repainted in gray, she sailed to Clydebank, the place of her birth, for refitting as a high-capacity troopship. She then made two more sailings to Canada, bringing servicemen over to Britain. In March 1940, she was dispatched to far-off waters, to New Zealand. Briefly, she sailed in convoy with the *Queen Mary*, the *Aquitania*, and other liner-troopers far removed from their peacetime runs. The *Empress*'s spell in southern climates was quite short, however.

The *Empress* was returning home to England, via Cape Town and Freetown, on October 26 when she was attacked and set afire by Nazi bombers. One of the bombs made a direct hit on the once splendid Mayfair Lounge. Sadly, she was only 70 miles north-west of Ireland at the time. She burned from end to end. All but forty-nine of her 600 passengers and crew were saved, however. The blistering hulk was finally put under tow by the Polish destroyer *Burza*, but two days later, on the 28th, the Nazi sub *U-32* sighted the former liner and fired two torpedoes. The once great *Empress* sank quickly. Some reports suggested that Hitler himself had ordered the ship to be sunk because of its association with the King, Queen, and their alliance-building North American trip a year-and-a-half before. In the final accounting, she became the largest Allied merchant ship to be lost in World War II.

When, after the war, in 1946, the British Government suggested that Canadian Pacific build another big Atlantic, a ship like the legendary *Empress of Britain*, the idea was politely declined. She had not been a profit-maker—she was too big. In future, within a decade or so following the war and not until the mid '50s, did Canadian Pacific again build big passenger ships. The 25,000-ton *Empress of Britain* and *Empress of England* were added in 1956–57 and later, in 1961, the 27,000-ton *Empress of Canada*. These ships were only more moderately sized and therefore more practical and profitable passenger ships.

Alone, however, the *Empress of Britain* of 1931 has left a long-lasting impression—one of a great, grand, and even romantic ocean liner. Additionally, her Canadian Pacific fleet mates—from the likes of the *Empress of Japan*, the *Empress of Russia*, the *Duchess of Richmond*, and the *Metagama*—create an interesting collection, reminders of nearly forgotten passenger ships. But hopefully, this book is a nostalgic review, a grand reminder, of Canadian Pacific liners between the wars.

The *Empress of Britain* departing from Canada with the royal couple onboard. (*Author's collection*)

War has begun: The *Empress of Britain* at Halifax in the fall of 1939. (*Canadian Pacific Steamships*)

Pitiful sight: The burning *Empress of Britain*. (*Author's collection*)

BIBLIOGRAPHY

Braynard, F. O., & Miller, W. H., *Fifty Famous Liners (Vol I)* (Cambridge, England: Patrick Stephens Ltd, 1982)

Harvey, C., *RMS Empress of Britain: Britain's Finest Liner* (Stroud, Gloucestershire, England: Tempus Publishing Ltd, 2004)

Haws, D., *Merchant Fleets: Canadian Pacific* (Hereford, England: TCL Publications, 1992)

Kludas, A., *Great Passenger Ships of the World, Vols I & II* (Cambridge, England: Patrick Stephens Ltd, 1972–73)

Streater, L., *The Canadian Empresses: A Chronology Volumes 1 & 2: 1889–1971* (United Kingdom: Maritime Publishing Concepts, 2009–2010)

Turner, R. D., *The Pacific Empresses* (Victoria, British Columbia: Sono Nis Press, 1981)